Monitoring the Impacts of Prison and Parole Services: An Initial Examination

LOUIS H. BLAIR
HARRY P. HATRY
KARAN BUNN
LESLIE STEVENS
KENNETH PARKER

A15043 397372

5039-2

July, 1977

THE URBAN INSTITUTE
WASHINGTON, D.C.

This research has been supported by the National Center for Productivity and Quality of Working Life, the State of North Carolina, and the State of Wisconsin. The recommendations are those of the authors and do not necessarily reflect the opinions of the supporting organizations.

The interpretations or conclusions are those of the authors and should not be attributed to The Urban Institute, its trustees, or to other organizations that support its research.

ISBN 87766-201-0

UI 5039-2

PLEASE REFER TO URI 16900 WHEN ORDERING

Available from:
Publications Office
The Urban Institute
2100 M Street, N.W.
Washington, D.C. 20037

List price: $3.95

A/77/3M

PREFACE

This report on procedures for monitoring prison and parole service outcomes is one of a series of reports about ways to measure the outcomes of basic state government services. The other reports deal with mental health, social services, chronic disease control programs, economic development, and transportation.

Concerned citizens and government officials—in particular, service agency personnel, budget and planning staffs, legislators, and gubernatorial staff—have become increasingly concerned about the effectiveness of government services. Little useful information is currently available on the effectiveness of such services in meeting the needs of their clientele. The research leading to this series of reports was, therefore, undertaken as an initial step toward developing procedures that would enable jurisdictions to obtain such information. Though the work was initially directed at helping state governments, the material also seems appropriate for local corrections agencies.

This series of reports is an initial effort in what is a very large task. Several of the procedures outlined in the reports need considerable development—steps that may require the investment of significant financial and staff resources. Despite its exploratory character, the work completed thus far indicates that considerably improved effectiveness information can be made available.

This work focuses on the outcomes (or end results) of services that a state or local agency should monitor and on the procedures for collecting data on these outcomes on a regular basis. Such data, collected over a period of time, can indicate trends, progress and problems. Consequently, outcome information is an important aid to public officials and concerned citizens for finding out just what is being accomplished and for identifying areas that need extensive examination.

These procedures are, however, no substitute for program evaluation methods (such as "controlled" experiments and sophisticated techniques of statistical analysis) that attempt to identify specific effects of specific programs.

The research that led to these reports was carried out by The Urban Institute and the states of North Carolina and Wisconsin, with the cooperation of the National Association of State Budget Officers. The National Center for Productivity and Quality of Working Life, the U.S. Department of Health, Education, and Welfare, the U.S. Department of Transportation, and the Ford Foundation provided financial support for these efforts.

We hope that these reports will increase awareness of the information needed to reflect citizen and client concerns regarding public services, encourage state and local governments to consider, develop, and use these or similar measurement procedures, and stimulate further research and developmental efforts to produce reliable outcome measurement techniques.

ACKNOWLEDGMENTS

This corrections effort was directed by Louis Blair of The Urban Institute. Major participants were Karan Bunn and Leslie Stevens of the North Carolina Division of State Budget; Kenneth Parker of the North Carolina Department of Corrections; and Harry Hatry of The Urban Institute, who was also the director of the overall project on performance measurement of selected state services.

The authors wish to thank the many people who offered suggestions and constructive criticisms, who provided insights into corrections programs and performance measurement, and who reviewed lengthy draft reports. Among the persons whose contributions we particularly want to acknowledge are Leonard Farrar, formerly of the North Carolina Division of State Planning; G. G. Williams, W. L. Kautzky, and J. H. Panton of the North Carolina Department of Correction; Gloria Grizzle and Kenneth Howard of the North Carolina Division of State Budget. All provided inputs to the effort at various key points in the project.

Paul H. Kusuda and Tom Heib, Wisconsin Division of Corrections, provided measurement ideas and detailed, extremely helpful suggestions on the various drafts; Bernard Mrazik, Wisconsin Department of Administration coordinated the effort in Wisconsin.

John Conrad, Academy for Contemporary Problems, gave detailed comments and posed stimulating questions that helped the authors make significant improvements in this report.

George Bell and J. Don Judy of the National Association of State Budget Officers provided numerous suggestions to help make the findings useful to all state governments.

The following provided helpful reviews of drafts of this report: Lawrence A. Greenfeld and W. R. Burkhart of the Law Enforcement Assistance Administration; George Cox, Georgia Department of Corrections; Chase Whittenburg, Maine Department of Mental Health and Corrections; Hugh H. Riddle, South Carolina Department of Corrections; Richard Erickson, Nebraska Department of Correction; Richard J. Oldroyd, Utah Division of Corrections; Kay Harris, American Bar Association Commission on Correctional Facilities and Services; and Virginia Wright, Henry Ruth, Thomas White, and Peter Block, The Urban Institute. Alfred Blumstein of Carnegie-Mellon University provided helpful suggestions on handling recidivism.

CONTENTS

EXHIBITS

EXECUTIVE SUMMARY

SCOPE

This report discusses procedures for regularly monitoring—at least annually, if possible—the effectiveness of state prison and parole services. Officials in the governor's office, the state budget office, and the state legislature, as well as the corrections agency, could use the information developed by such procedures for several purposes:

- To assess the progress correctional services are making in meeting a variety of goals, including holding inmates securely and humanely, and reducing subsequent criminal activity;
- To help determine priorities in resource allocation and justify the needs for resources or activities;
- To identify particular problem areas for in-depth study to determine alternate solutions and their costs;
- To increase the accountability of government services to the public and to elected officials.

Exhibit 1 lists measures suggested for regular monitoring. These constitute a starting point for obtaining regular performance information; they are not intended to be the final word on measurement. Some of these measures have major limitations; yet the information these or similar measures can yield is important for informed decision making.

This overview of opportunities for measuring corrections outcomes is intended to help top executive and legislative officials make decisions on the type of measurement procedures to develop. The body of the report, which discusses the suggested measurement and data-collection procedures in detail, is intended more for analysts and evaluators.

APPROACH

This report is based on a relatively small research effort involving

1. An examination of measures state corrections agencies currently use to monitor the effects of their prison and parole activities on offenders and on the public. The examination included a telephone survey of forty-six state corrections agencies; site visits to two states, North Carolina and Wisconsin; a review of budgets from all states; and a review of reports of corrections departments in more than thirty states.

2. Identification of specific measures and the necessary data-collection procedures state corrections agencies might use as a basis for monitoring. Procedures that can provide rapid feedback (at relatively low costs) on performance of some of the more important aspects of prison and parole services are emphasized, along with measures covering the whole prison and parole population—not just offenders treated by special programs.

3. Limited tests of a few measurement procedures to identify difficulties likely to be encountered; to suggest operational definitions of terms, approaches to be used, and steps to be followed; and to determine the approximate amount of time and effort required for the measurement activities. The testing, as well as much of the earlier identification, was carried out jointly by the North Carolina Department of Correction and Divisions of State Budget and of Planning.

Exhibit 1

SUGGESTED OBJECTIVES AND MEASURES FOR MONITORING PRISON AND PAROLE SERVICES

OBJECTIVES: Incarcerate offenders securely so that they cannot inflict harm on the public, while also providing for the safety, humane treatment, and health of inmates
Rehabilitate offenders so that they do not commit criminal offenses when released to the community and assist them in becoming socially productive and integrated into the community.

Objective Characteristic	Measures	Principal Data Breakouts	Data Collection Means/Source
To hold securely	1. Annual number of *escapes* divided by annual Average Daily Population (ADP)	Level of security, facility	Analysis of existing escape and prison population records
	2. Number of *crimes committed against the public* ascribed to escapees and to inmates on authorized absence (e.g., work release)	Type of offense, security level	Escape and recapture records and inmate files
	3. Number of incidents of *failure of internal* security, by type of incident, total divided by ADP	Level of security, facility	Special report
	a. Incidents involving *contraband*	Type of contraband	
	b. Incidents of *unrest* by groups of inmates	Type of unrest	
	c. Physical *assaults on prison officials*		
	d. Physical *assaults on inmates* requiring medical treatment		
To hold humanely	4. Number of inmate-days of *overcrowding*	Facility	Analysis of existing records
	5. Rating of *sanitation conditions* in facilities	Facility	Trained observer inspections
	6. Percentage of inmates with unmet health needs	Major facility	Physical examination of a sample of inmates
To rehabilitate (changes in attitude)	7. Percentages of inmates with substantial improvement-degradation in attitude associated with criminal or social behavior based on psychological test scales administered at intake and at release; numbers of scales showing significant improvement-degradation	Client-difficulty level	MMPI tests or other psychological exams of random sample of inmates at intake and at discharge
To rehabilitate (reduction in criminal activity)	8. *Criminal involvement while under parole*	Client-difficulty level	State criminal justice information network, corrections intake records, FBI RAP sheet follow-up on random sample of parolees
	a. Percentage of all offenders on parole in the past 12 months who are *arrested* (or whose arrest passes a preliminary hearing) for a criminal offense allegedly committed prior to completion of parole, or		
	b. Percentage of all offenders on parole in the past 12 months who are *convicted* of a criminal offense that was committed while on parole; or		
	c. Percentage of all offenders who successfully complete parole *without revocation* for a criminal offense		

Objective Characteristic	Measures	Principal Data Breakouts	Data Collection Means/Source

	9. *Criminal involvement when no longer under supervision*
	  a. Percentage of offenders *arrested* (or whose arrest passes a preliminary hearing) for a criminal offense within 12 months of completion of parole or unconditional discharge; or
	  b. Percentage of offenders *convicted* for a criminal offense committed within 12 months of completion of parole or unconditional discharge; or
	  c. Percentage of offenders *reincarcerated* for a criminal offense within 12 months of completion of parole or unconditional discharge
		Client-difficulty level	State criminal justice information network, corrections intake records, FBI RAP sheet follow-up on random sample of former inmates

	10. *Reincarceration:* Number and percentage of offenders entering prison who have previously been incarcerated in the state prison system		Corrections agency records, FBI RAP sheets, court records
To rehabilitate (increase in social productivity)	11. Percentage of ex-offenders *employed* or otherwise socially productive full time when released from parole	Client employment-difficulty level	Parole agent reports, or special tracking of sample about to be released

ASSUMED CORRECTIONS OBJECTIVES

The measures suggested in this report are derived from a general statement of corrections objectives similar to statements that many state governments and corrections agencies have adopted. It includes two basic objectives:

- To hold in a secure and humane manner offenders sentenced to incarceration by the courts; and
- To rehabilitate offenders so that they will not commit criminal offenses when released to the community, and to help them become socially productive and integrated into the community.

Rehabilitation is not universally recognized as an achievable objective for a corrections agency, and thus it is sometimes considered inappropriate to try to measure rehabilitation. There also appears to be little evidence that corrections efforts have been able to achieve rehabilitation. Nonetheless, as long as state legislatures and the public expect it, and as long as corrections agencies provide a substantial amount of services intended to rehabilitate offenders, it seems appropriate to measure rehabilitation. But the measurement may then only document the inability to achieve rehabilitation (at least with existing correctional programs) and thus provide evidence leading to changes in objectives or programs.

FINDINGS AND PROPOSED MEASUREMENT PROCEDURES

As summarized in exhibit 1, eleven basic measures are suggested. These measures indicate the outcomes of state activities. They do not identify specific steps to correct unsatisfactory conditions. Corrective steps might require action by the legislature or the governor's office, as well as by the corrections agency.

Four types of data-collection procedures or sources are needed for these measures: (1) records typically kept by corrections agencies or data that corrections officials can report readily; (2) records of criminal activities for random samples of released offenders; (3) physical and psychological examinations of a random sample of inmates; and (4) inspections of prison facilities. The principal measures and associated data-collection procedures that appear needed fall into four groups:

1. *Measurements of internal security (Measures 1–3, Chapter II)*

These include measures of escape rates (Measure 1); crimes by escapees or inmates on authorized absence (Measure 2); and frequencies of contraband incidents, inmate assaults on officials and on other inmates, and incidents of unrest (Measure 3). Although individual incidents are often recorded somewhere in the system—most likely at the unit level—they are seldom tallied and divided by the average daily population (ADP) at each level of security to facilitate comparisons over time and among facilities. The diversity of definitions the various correctional facilities within the state use for terms such as unrest and assault will also affect accuracy. Suggestions for standardized definitions, a reporting format, and data collection procedures are provided in Chapter II.

2. *Measurements of "humane" incarceration (Measures 4–6, Chapter II)*

Court rulings and a growing awareness of civil rights entitling inmates to a reasonable degree of humane treatment have given added importance to this area. Currently there is virtually no regular reporting of information on humane treatment. A measure which apparently is not reported in any state but is readily available is the degree of overcrowding of facilities using inmate-days of overcrowding, the annual sum of daily overcrowding as measured by the number of inmates housed in excess of current facility capacity (Measure 4). It might require some effort to determine *actual* current "capacity" of each facility.

At least twenty-four states inspect sanitation, health, or fire conditions in prison facilities, but the inspections vary greatly in scope and frequency. There was not enough time to develop a model inspection system nor to review all existing prison inspection procedures, but the development and implementation of a comprehensive procedure for determining, at least annually, health and sanitation conditions at each facility are suggested (Measure 5).

Inmates suffer from many illnesses and have incidence rates substantially higher than the general population for hypertension, genito-urinary tract infections, and malnutrition. No state corrections agency is known to monitor routinely the health of inmates who have been incarcerated for a substanial amount of time (for example, at least six months), although many give physical exams at intake. Only one state, Michigan, is known to have conducted a comprehensive physical

examination of inmate health *after* intake, but this effort has not been repeated. The health status of inmates, in terms of the percentage with unmet medical needs (Measure 6), can be estimated by a physical examination of a randomly selected sample of as few as 100 to 200 inmates from the entire prison population. The examination could be conducted with contract medical personnel for approximately $100 per inmate. Use of state health department personnel could greatly cut out-of-pocket costs.

3. *A proxy rehabilitation measure: the change in attitude of offenders during incarceration (Measure 7, Chapter II)*

Many corrections agencies administer a battery of psychological examinations at intake, often using the Minnesota Multiphasic Personality Inventory (MMPI). No corrections agency is known to administer tests regularly at both intake and release and complile aggregate statistics to estimate overall changes. The suggested measure involves administering a standardized psychological test just prior to realease to a random sample of as few as 100 to 200 inmates who took the same test when they entered incarceration. The pre- and postincarceration scores of the sample (especially of subsets of scores particularly related to criminal or antisocial behavior) would then be compared to determine changes during incarceration. This measurement procedure is currently being tested by the North Carolina Department of Correction. Much time and effort might be required to validate this measure, that is, to relate changes in test scores to subsequent behavior.

4. *Measurements of criminal activity and social productivity after release from incarceration (Measures 8–11, Chapter III)*

Of particular interest to citizens and legislatures is the amount of crime the offenders commit after release from prison. Two measures are suggested, one for criminal activities while on parole (Measure 8) and one for criminal activities after release from all correctional supervision to determine longer term outcomes of corrections services (Measure 9).

It is very hard to measure criminal activity accurately because only a small proportion of crimes committed (typically less than 20 percent) ever result in conviction or even arrest. Several different indicators of continued criminal activity can be used: arrests, or, preferably, "quality arrests" (those that have passed a preliminary hearing); convictions; and reincarcerations.

The measures most frequently used are based on reincarceration within the same state—and usually only for an offense committed while still on parole. Although such reincarceration reporting is commendable, it underestimates criminal activity by omitting subsequent arrests or convictions in other states (FBI data indicate that about half of the recidivists have arrests in more than one state), arrests that do not lead to convictions, convictions that do not lead to incarceration, and, in some states, criminal activity *after* leaving parole.

However, data collection is much harder for a measure based on arrests or on convictions than for one based on reincarcerations. Arrest data, including out-of-state and federal arrests and sometimes convictions data, are available from the FBI Identification Records Division Reporting System on "RAP" sheets (though some states have had difficulty obtaining the data in a timely way). Within-state arrests and convictions are available in some states from a criminal justice information system. Recidivism statistics could be developed from the FBI RAP sheets for a sample of 300 offenders with perhaps one to two person-months of effort. Recidivism measures based on RAP sheet data are not currently generated periodically by any state corrections agency, but several states and the U.S. Bureau of Prisons have used them for special studies.

A readily available, but crude, proxy measure for rehabilitation (and an indicator of the difficulty of rehabilitating offenders) is the number or percentage of offenders entering prison in the past year who had had previous incarcerations (Measure 10). This type of measure is used regularly by twenty-six states.

However, the reincarceration measure falls far short of providing a full perspective on recidivism. The measure does not indicate the percentage of all persons receiving corrections services that return to crime. For example, a three-year follow-up study of offenders released in North Carolina showed that although 80 percent had been rearrested, and 73 percent reconvicted, only 33 percent had been reincarcerated for fifteen days or more. Therefore, before relying solely on reincarceration data to measure recidivism, a state should also compare the data on arrests and convictions with the reincarceration data on a sample of ex-offenders, to estimate, albeit crudely, the extent to which reincarcerations underestimate known criminal activity.

Prison or parole services often try to enhance the employability or general social productivity of offenders. Records kept by parole officers often contain data on employment, income, and other aspects of parolees' lives. Only two states, however, apparently summarize these data for all parolees. Values for the percentage of ex-offenders employed or otherwise socially productive when released from parole (Measure 11) can probably be obtained relatively easily if parole records are up-to-date and accurate. If these records are not accurate, a much more tedious check on a sample of 100 to 200 offenders leaving parole each year would have to be conducted. Measuring social productivity for persons after they have completed parole or have been discharged unconditionally does not appear practical because of the difficulties in locating and interviewing them. Moreover, officials in some states may feel that the possibly unwarranted invasion of privacy would make such follow-ups inappropriate for any monitoring effort.

Annual statistics should be subdivided, if possible, by "client difficulty"—the estimated difficulty of rehabilitating the particular sets of offenders released. This categorization can help officials determine if any changes are due to differences in the mix of offenders being released. A few states now use "base expectancy" scores, which attempt to predict the likelihood of recidivism based primarily on offender characteristics such as previous criminal history. These scores could also be used to help classify offenders as to client difficulty.

IMPLEMENTATION AND COST/STAFF TIME REQUIREMENTS

Implementation of these measurements will involve deciding which measures and which particular forms of the measures are most appropriate (this report identifies some possible forms with pros and cons of each); assessing the adequacy of current information; establishing new data-collection and reporting procedures or modifying existing ones; developing or modifying analysis and data-processing procedures and specifying output formats; and reviewing procedures with prison and parole officials and obtaining approval for changes. The amount of effort and time required for implementation can vary greatly according to the number of measures to be implemented, the number of similar data-collection procedures that already exist, the ease with which data in current records can be extracted, the size of the system, the number of facilities for which individual data are desired, and the willingness and interest of corrections officials at all levels to gather and report data on individual incidents and offenders.

At a minimum, *initial* implementation of the basic definitions and development of appropriate procedures for most of the measures (all except Measure 5, sanitation conditions, and Measure 6, physical health), would probably take a total of at least twelve to twenty-four person-months of staff time. As some of these measures have not been tested, these are only crude estimates. An additional minimum of six to twelve months would probably be required for implementing Measures 5 and 6.

The efforts required for *annual* data collection, after all of the measures and data collection procedures have been worked out in detail, can also be estimated only crudely. Much depends on the quality of the existing information system, the data-processing capability, and the size of the corrections agency. A minimum of ten person-months of staff effort annually is expected to be necessary for collecting data for all but Measures 5 and 6 once the basic procedures have been implemented. An additional six to ten person-months of corrections staff time, plus a substantial amount of staff time of state health department personnel and $20,000 to $75,000, dependent on the number of inmates requiring physical examinations, would be required for Measures 5 and 6.

FUTURE RESEARCH NEEDS

This initial examination of outcome monitoring for state prison and parole activities has been very limited. Not all of the relevant research topics have been fully explored, nor have many of the procedures been tested adequately. Specific items appropriate for continued research, whether by individual states or preferably on a national basis, include the following:

1. *Additional testing of this proposed monitoring system*

Particular attention would be devoted to determining the costs, accuracy, and feasibility of the data-collection procedures; documenting the actual steps taken to collect the monitoring data; and validating the measures. In late 1976, the North Carolina Department of Correction was testing some of the measures. Their experiences and findings regarding the value of the measures should be useful to other corrections agencies contemplating this type of performance monitoring. Additional time and effort are necessary to validate some of the measures—for example, how do psychological test scores taken during incarceration relate to changes in subsequent criminal behavior?

2. *Additional research on recidivism measurement*

If corrections has an objective of reducing criminal activity after release, then recidivism is one of the most important of all performance aspects to measure, but the validity of the measure—whether arrests or "quality" arrests, convictions, or reincarcerations are used—remains uncertain. Research is needed to test the validity of alternative forms of the measure and to determine which specific recidivism measure, with a reasonable collection cost, comes closest to providing valid, accurate data on continued criminal activity and to facilitating year-to-year comparisons.

3. *Development of a survey instrument for inmates on prison conditions and quality of services*

It seems desirable to obtain offender opinions on the quality of corrections services, particularly at, or shortly after, release from incarceration and from parole. "Clients" have a different, yet important, perspective, and data probably can be collected relatively easily and inexpensively. Corrections officials may question whether unwilling and frequently bitter clients give honest answers to controversial questions. Nonetheless, an effort to develop, and, if possible, validate, a survey approach seems appropriate. A survey of persons just released from prison and possibly one for persons just released from parole would yield systematic feedback on their perceptions of such corrections system characteristics as internal security, sanitary conditions, and rehabilitation efforts. Focusing on changes in the ratings over time is likely to provide more meaningful information.

4. *Development of a standard procedure for inspection of prison facilities*

Twenty-four states reported inspecting correctional facilities, but the scope and frequency of the inspections varied greatly—from occasional walk-throughs by the warden with no written criteria or check lists, to periodic inspections by sanitation, health, and fire personnel using written criteria and assigning numerical ratings. An examination of the inspection operations of various states, and the development and testing of an inspections procedure giving quantitative, reliable ratings on conditions affecting the health and safety of inmates are needed.

5. *Development of additional measures for incarceration*

Some states may be interested in additional measures for such areas as humane treatment (quality of opportunities for meaningful work or educational and vocational services in the prison; provision of clean clothing and bedding; adequacy of food; behavior of guards; prompt medical care), the deterrent effects of incarceration (on others), or equity in punishment. These become particularly important if the emphasis in correctional services shifts from rehabilitation to incarceration. Because of the limited resources available, this study has not focused on developing such measures, but has stayed within the somewhat more traditional corrections objectives. (Some tentative suggestions are presented in Appendix A.)

6. *Developing measures of social functioning and community adaptation*

Many corrections agencies have an objective of achieving social reintegration of the offender. Yet there are no reliable indicators, expect for "social productivity," to measure achievement in this area. There is some relevant research in the social services area, as well as relevant activity in Wisconsin and New York state corrections agencies. Appendix A presents some initial thoughts on possible options for further development and testing.

CHAPTER I

INTRODUCTION AND CORRECTIONS OBJECTIVES

STUDY PURPOSE

The purpose of this report is to present some measurement procedures that a state government could use to assess systematically its adult prison and parole services and the progress of the state government in meeting correctional goals. If data on these measures can be collected and reported regularly, the resulting information should help officials in the corrections agency, the state budget and planning offices, the governor's office, and the state legislature.

Measurement data on the outcomes of corrections services have a number of uses, including the following:

- To assess the overall progress that the corrections agency is making. This knowledge is important to top officials in the corrections agency as well as to officials in the governor's office and in the legislature who are responsible for corrections services.
- To provide help in determining budget allocations and, when appropriate, justifying the need for additional resources, facilities, or activities. Inadequacies in performance such as overcrowding, inadequate health care, and unsanitary facilities which clearly cannot be met with current resources can be documented, thereby perhaps increasing the likelihood of additional funding.

- To help establish priorities for corrective actions. Many states no doubt have various deficiencies in corrections services. Indicating where these are and their extent should facilitate systematic planning and allocation of resources.
- To increase the accountability of corrections services to the legislature, to the governor, to the budget office, and to the general public. Measurement procedures provide criteria by which officials can be held responsible.
- To provide information for program evaluations, performance audits, zero-based budgeting, management by objectives, and any other management systems concerned with the performance of correction programs.

Presenting the measurements annually (and possibly more frequently) can prompt the agency to take appropriate corrective action and enable effects of such actions to be assessed relatively quickly. The measurement procedures, and in some cases the data, are also likely to be useful for special studies such as in-depth evaluations to determine if any cause-effect relationships exist in specific correctional programs.

This study has concentrated on developing measurement procedures for monitoring adult prison and parole services. Some of the procedures probably also can be modified readily for use in monitoring probation services and adapted to cover juvenile services.

Still others could be used for monitoring jail services.

These procedures are not presented as definitive but as a starting point for corrections, budget, and legislative officials to develop and implement a set of measures appropriate for their own states. Each state may, for example, want to develop additional "operationally oriented" measures for use by wardens or other officials within a prison unit to monitor conditions under their control.

For the most part, the information obtainable from the measurement procedures will not indicate the specific actions needed to correct problems revealed by the data. To correct a particular problem, a special effort will probably be required to determine causes, possible corrective actions, and costs and effects. What, then, is the use of measures that don't tell corrections officials what to do? They already know there are problems in virtually every aspect of corrections services because they have to handle too many offenders and feel the legislature does not provide enough resources. The authors believe that such "performance" information is essential for informed decision making and for planning and establishing priorities, particularly when there are not enough resources to meet all of the needs.

OBJECTIVES FOR CORRECTIONS

Traditionally it has been assumed that crime and the criminal's impact on society can be reduced if corrections—as part of the whole criminal justice system—can achieve certain objectives. This study has taken a set of four objectives as the starting point for discussion and development of measures of outcome:

Objective 1. To incarcerate offenders securely so that they cannot inflict harm on the public, while also providing for the safety, humane treatment, and health of inmates.

Objective 2. To rehabilitate offenders so that they do not commit criminal offenses when released to the community; to assist them in becoming socially productive and integrated into the community.

Objective 3. To deter would-be offenders; to prevent crime.

Objective 4. To exact retribution; to punish the offenders.

Emphasis among these has varied over time. A century or more ago, the most important objective seemed to be punishment; then came the emphases on deterrence and rehabilitation. Recently, some have suggested that rehabilitation attempts generally are, and for many reasons will continue to be, failures, and that rehabilitation is not so much the responsibility of the corrections agency as of society. Emphasis may therefore be shifting from rehabilitation to incarcerating offenders to prevent them from committing further crimes against the public while they serve out their sentences.[1]

It has been argued by some in the corrections field that one of these four objectives, rehabilitation, cannot be achieved by a corrections agency, that it is not an appropriate objective, and thus it should not be measured.[2] Officials in many states, however, feel that rehabilitation is a valid objective. States offer vocational, educational, and counseling services to offenders in the hope that offenders will not commit crimes when released to the community. Some states have in their budgets or annual reports explicit objectives on rehabilitating offenders or changing their behavior so that they do not commit crimes after release from all correctional supervision. Therefore, it seems appropriate, if not necessary, for states to attempt to measure the extent of rehabilitation, and at least twenty-five states have such measures. In this study, measures for the rehabilitation objective have been included for use by states that believe it to be an appropriate objective.[3]

---

1. Objectives and goals have been stated in many different ways. This set of four is based on the statements of Donald R. Cressey, "Adult Felons in Prison," *Prisoners in America*. A similar listing of functions as well as a number of negative, inadvertent objectives has been developed by C. E. Reasons and R. L. Kaplan, "Tear Down the Walls? Some Functions of Prison," *Crime and Delinquency,* October 1975, pp. 360–372. We have not, however, suggested any measures for these inadvertent objectives.

2. See John P. Conrad, "Fifty Years in a Squirrel Cage, The Past, Present, and Future of Evaluation in Corrections"; Paul E. Lehman, "A Medical Model of Treatment," *Crime and Delinquency,* 18 (2); John P. Conrad, "Never Should Have Promised a Hospital," *Federal Probation,* Dec. 1975; James Q. Wilson, "Lock 'Em Up and Other Thoughts on Crime," *New York Times Magazine,* March 9, 1975. An article which points out the apparent impossibility of corrections services to reduce recidivism is Robert Martinson, "What Works?—A Question and Answer About Prison Reform," *Public Interest,* Spring, 1974, pp. 22–54. Martinson's article is based on an examination of evaluations of a number of corrections programs conducted in the 1950s and 1960s, which has been analyzed in Lipton, Martinson, and Wilks, *The Effectiveness of Correctional Treatment.*

3. If, in fact, rehabilitation is *not* an achievable objective, then the sooner states are convinced of it, the sooner resources can be allocated more wisely. Accurate information on rehabilitation failure in each state—which could be obtained in part with these suggested measures—might help states modify their objectives and their programs. It must be pointed out that past failures do not necessarily mean rehabilitation is impossible. At least for some categories of offenders, certain types of correctional assistance may in the future turn out to have some beneficial effect. See, for example, K. J. Lenihan, "When Money Counts."

It should be noted that actions taken by a corrections agency to improve performance in one objective may lead to reduced performance in meeting another objective. For example, keeping inmates under tight security, thereby denying them work-release programs, should reduce the number of escapes and the crimes committed while escaped or on authorized absence (Objective 1), but might also result in greater difficulty for offenders in obtaining jobs or being socially productive on release (Objective 2). Also, corrections is an instrument of the courts in exacting retribution and in deterring crime; the courts, in setting sentences, may have more influence than corrections in determining the extent to which Objectives 3 and 4 are achieved.

Development of measures for Objectives 1 and 2 has received priority here because these are the objectives that many corrections systems have accepted, explicitly or otherwise, and around which they have developed programs. Measuring performance on the deterrence and retribution objectives appears to require special studies rather than regular performance monitoring.

Each of the four objectives is discussed further below.

Objective 1. To incarcerate offenders securely so that they cannot inflict harm on the public, while also providing for the safety, humane treatment, and health of inmates.

The corrections agency is expected to control offenders sentenced to incarceration by the courts so that they do not commit additional crimes against the public during the period of their sentences. Courts and the corrections community have strongly suggested that incarceration means not only holding offenders securely, but also providing humane treatment. Humane treatment has been defined in part by the American Correctional Association[4] and the National Advisory Commission on Criminal Justice Standards and Goals (NACCJSG)[5] as meeting health needs, providing protection to prison officials and to offenders, and providing adequate food, shelter, and clothing. There also seems to be agreement that prisons should be run in an orderly fashion, with adequate discipline and security to avoid incidents of violence—riots, crimes against other offenders, assaults on guards, and so forth.

---

4. Extracted from Principles VI and XXIII of the "Declaration of Principles of the American Correctional Association, Revised and Reaffirmed in 1960."

5. Extracted from Standards 2.4, 2.5, and 2.6 of National Advisory Commission on Criminal Justice Standards and Goals (NACCJSG), *Corrections.*

Officials in various states may feel that offenders should be offered meaningful opportunities for work, self-development, or preparation for life after prison, for recreation and education programs, and for filling otherwise idle hours. There is probably substantial merit to these contentions, from a humane standpoint and possibly from a rehabilitation standpoint. Because of time and resource limitations, however, this study concentrated on developing measures of basic conditions during incarceration rather than what might be called amenities. Additional proposed measures for humane treatment are discussed in Appendix A.

Objective 2. To rehabilitate offenders so that they do not commit criminal offenses when released to the community; to assist them in becoming socially productive and integrated with the community.

Many corrections agencies attempt to rehabilitate offenders in at least two ways: through specific programs to increase offenders' ability to stay away from crime and to cope legitimately upon release as well as through the threat of later incarceration either by parole revocation or by a new conviction. Despite the serious questions as to whether corrections can change offenders, the public and legislative interest in rehabilitation and the amount of effort many states spend on it seem to justify systematic monitoring of this objective. The objective can be examined in terms of reduction in continued criminal activity (recidivism, however that term is defined), as well as through employment performance and social adjustment after incarceration. These latter aspects not only might affect recidivism, but also are important in their own right. Offender rehabilitation needs to be monitored not only while offenders are on parole, but also—so far as is possible—after they complete parole and no longer face the immediate threat of reincarceration through parole revocation. Because of difficulties in locating ex-offenders and the problem of intruding on the privacy of persons who have "paid their debts" to society, postcorrection performance can probably be monitored regularly only through recidivism rates and not through employment success or social adjustment.

Objective 3. To deter would-be offenders; to prevent crime.

The unpleasantness of correctional control—particularly incarceration—is intended to deter would-be offenders from committing crimes. Actions of the entire criminal justice system and the criminal apprehension component—and not corrections alone—affect deterrence. Moreover, incarcerating offenders eliminates the crimes which these persons, if free, might be inflicting on the public. Incarceration may, however, increase the amount of postincarceration crime. Although it is important to examine the role of corrections in deterring would-be offenders, this task appears to be beyond the scope of state corrections agencies for annual monitoring and would be more appropriate in special studies of the impacts of the criminal justice system. Monitoring of this objective is discussed briefly in Appendix A.

Objective 4. To exact retribution; to punish offenders.

Retribution has been a traditional objective for treating persons judged to be guilty—make the offenders pay the price for their crimes, generally through incarceration for the more severe offenses. For each type of crime, the equity of punishment can be measured by the length and type of sentence—factors which are affected by the court's initial sentence, although a corrections agency can often influence the length of time served by its recommendations to the paroling authority. This objective seems to apply more to the courts and parole authorities which control the length of the sentence than to the corrections agency. This report proposes no measurement procedures for annual monitoring of this objective.

CRITERIA FOR SELECTING MEASURES OF THE EFFECTS OF CORRECTIONS

The proposed measures of correction outcome try to indicate how much progress, if any, the corrections agency is making toward meeting the stated objectives. The emphasis is on developing practical, economical measures for collecting data regularly and reporting findings at least annually. Some measures which entail demanding, cumbersome, or expensive data-collection procedures or which require extensive development of procedures (such as physical examinations of a sample of inmates or inspection of prison facilities) would be conducted only for samples of offenders or for particular facilities in the corrections system.

Criteria for assisting in the selection of individual measures are discussed below. A measure might be rated low on one or more criteria but still be included because of its overall importance. (See exhibit 2 for a tentative assessment of these measures.)

1. *Importance*—The measure covers an important aspect of corrections services, prison conditions, or rehabilitation. The aspect being examined contributes substantially to the achievement of one of the stated objectives.
2. *Uniqueness*—No other measure provides the same information.
3. *Validity*—The value of the measure or changes in

its value over time clearly indicate a degree of achievement—or lack of it—in meeting one or more aspects of the stated objectives.
4. *"Influenceable"*—The corrections agency can change its operations or facilities in a way that will substantially influence or affect the value of a measure, although additional funding might be required. (*Complete* control over the value of the measure would not be a reasonable criterion.)[6]
5. *Precision/Reliability*—The data source is reliable. Changes and trends can be calculated with confidence that they indicate what is really happening to the value of the measure.
6. *Timeliness*—*Measurement* data can be made available soon enough for the government to use them meaningfully in making policy or resource allocation decisions.
7. *Reasonable Costs and Manpower Requirements*—The data can be collected and processed on a regular basis at "reasonable" costs, without undue strain on corrections employees, and without curtailment or disruption of other necessary corrections activities. (However, special training or the use of technical consultants might be required.)

Measures of efficiency (such as dollars expended per inmate-year) have not been included, nor have measures of work accomplished (such as inmates received or handled, or medical examinations given). Efficiency and work accomplished are important for management control purposes, but in themselves say little about the effectiveness of corrections activities and the extent to which corrections objectives are being achieved. (These data should, however, be considered in a comprehensive system of performance measurement.) Measures of benefit-cost relationships have not been suggested because of the problem of accurately translating benefits into monetary values. Measures of the profitability of various prison industries were omitted because the success or failure of such endeavors does not appear to be related directly to the proposed objectives.

---

6. Some readers may feel that the application of this criterion would eliminate the recidivism measures. They would probably agree with Cressey, "Adult Felons in Prison," p. 148, who maintains that ". . . high recidivism rates should not be regarded as the responsibility of the last institution to deal with the offender. No institution reviewing the men made 'failures' by the rest of society should be expected to make 'successes' of a very large portion of them. Also prisons cannot properly be given credit for those who commit no crimes after imprisonment. Committing first offenses and persistence in crime are all determined principally by conditions other than institutional policies and programs." We strongly suggest that recidivism measures be used but that officials recognize limitations with such measures.

Exhibit 2
ASSESSMENTS OF SUGGESTED MEASURES
(H=High; M=Medium; L=Low)

Specific Measure	Importance	Uniqueness	Validity	Influenceable	Precision/ Reliability	Timeliness	Costs/ Manpower
1. Escapes	H	H	H	H	H	H	L
2. Crimes by escapees	M–L	H	M–L	M	M	H	L
3. Failure of internal security	H	H	M–L	M–L	M	H	L
4. Overcrowding	H	H	H	H?	H	H	L
5. Sanitation conditions	H	H	M–H	H?	H?	H	M–H
6. Percentage needing medical care	M–H	H	M–H	H?	M	M	H
7. Change in attitude	M–L	M(8, 9)	M–L	?	M?	H	M–H
8. & 9. Recidivism:							
Parole completion	H	H	M?	L	H	H	L
Arrests	H	H	M–L?	L	M	M–L	M–H
Convictions	H	H	M–L?	L	H	L	M
10. Reincarcerations	M	M(8, 9)	M	L	H	H	L
11. Employment and social productivity	M–H	H	M–H	L–M	M	L–M	H

Explanation of Assessment Criteria

Importance

High	Essential item of information; collect even if expensive.
Medium	Desirable item of information; might be a special need or interest in it.
Low	Collect only if very inexpensive, if a special problem exists.

Uniqueness

High	No information on this aspect from any other measure in this set.
Medium	Similar information from other measures (See Measures 8 and 9).
Low	Virtually same information as from another measure. (No measures with low rating were suggested.)

Validity

High	Measure directly covers the aspect or an important facet of it (other measures might be needed to cover other facets).
Medium	Does not cover completely but value of the measure appears closely related to achievement of objective.
Low	Value of measure indicates something about performance but hard to interpret or to relate to performance.

Influenceable

High	Can exercise virtually total control over value.
Medium	Can exercise substantial control, but other factors are not controllable.
Low	Corrections has little control over it.

Precision/Reliability

High	No question on accuracy.
Medium	Some question, but probably accurate enough for most uses.
Low	Probably should not be used without validation data from other sources.

Timeliness

High	Can detect any differences within 3 months.
Medium	Can probably detect differences within 3 to 12 months.
Low	Will probably take more than a year for measure to reflect differences caused by corrections action.

Costs and Manpower for Data Collection or Analysis (after procedures have been developed.)

High	Probably in excess of 1 person-year of professional or analytic staff time or $15,000 additional expenditures for professional services.
Medium	Perhaps 3 to 12 person-months of professional or analytic staff time or corresponding expenditure for professional service.
Low	Less than 3 person-months.

RESEARCH APPROACH

The research for this effort to develop measurement tools involved three basic elements:

1. *A review of the existing literature* on corrections evaluation and research findings, of state corrections agencies' reports, and of state budgets. Included are evaluations of specific treatment programs, reviews of types of evaluations that have been conducted, and publications covering the mechanics of evaluating correctional programs. Reports from corrections, sections of state budgets, annual reports, and special studies by state corrections agencies were reviewed to determine some of the specific measures for which data are periodically collected and presented.[7]

2. *A telephone survey of state correction agencies* to determine what outcome measurement practices were being used in the individual states. For the most part, this survey consisted of semistructured interviews with the head of the office responsible for research and evaluation or planning. Corrections or criminal justice personnel in forty-five states and the District of Columbia were interviewed.[8] Findings relating to specific measurement procedures are presented in the discussions of the individual measures.

3. *The development of measures with North Carolina and Wisconsin corrections officials.* This part of the project, focused on incarceration-related measures in North Carolina, comprises the major part of the entire work. Tentative objectives and measures for regular monitoring were proposed, discussed, and reviewed in considerable detail with North Carolina officials in the Divisions of State Budget and State Planning, the Research and Evaluation Office of the Department of Correction, and the Division of Prisons.

The Wisconsin Division of Corrections had a substantial research effort underway in conjunction with a study to determine how best to classify parolees and probationers and how to assign staff to the in-community rehabilitation effort. A number of discussions took place covering the postincarceration rehabilitation and social functioning of ex-offenders.

---

7. Many of these findings are reported in Chapter III of *The Status of Productivity Measurement in State Government,* a report for the National Center for Productivity and Quality of Working Life, prepared by The Urban Institute in cooperation with the National Association of State Budget Officers. Some of the reports likely to be useful to corrections agencies are listed in the bibliography of that work.

8. Alaska, Hawaii, New Hampshire, North Carolina, and Wisconsin were not included in the telephone interviews.

SOME GENERAL FINDINGS FROM THE TELEPHONE SURVEY ON CURRENT EVALUATION AND MONITORING ACTIVITIES IN STATE CORRECTIONS AGENCIES

State corrections agencies devote much energy to measurement and evaluation activities, including the following:

- *Identification of population movement and population characteristics.* These studies indicate the numbers and types of offenders handled by the corrections agency and provide demographic data (such as age, race, county of commitment, education, and type of offense), but they tell virtually nothing about corrections effectiveness.

- *Special program evaluations.* These studies generally evaluate selected groups of offenders—for example, those who have gone through special programs such as work release or vocational rehabilitation. Because they are usually only one-time evaluation efforts, year-to-year comparisons to determine changes in performance are generally not possible.

- *Monitoring of performance.* Some attention has been devoted to monitoring performance. Some fifteen states have periodically measured a few aspects of performance—usually recidivism, employment, or social productivity—or conducted program evaluations. The performance indicators found most frequently are measures of parole revocation rates and other measures of recidivism (defined in many ways). Corrections agencies in fourteen states reported recidivism statistics annually. There is relatively little reporting of conditions in prisons (other than sanitation inspections), and few measures of offenders' behavior in prison. Findings are generally reported by an office of "research and evaluation," "statistics," or "planning." Reasons cited by officials interviewed in states with little monitoring of performance included "no personnel," "no automated data processing," or "the research and evaluation office has just been established." Those approaches which appeared applicable to other states have been adapted for use in this report.

No state was found to have a comprehensive capability to measure both the incarceration and in-community characteristics recommended here. Most of the measures described, however, have been used by at least one state corrections agency, though not necessarily on a regular basis. Many persons in the research and evaluation offices expressed a need for additional measurement approaches. The following chapters try to provide such suggestions.

CHAPTER II

MEASURES FOR MONITORING INCARCERATION

In this chapter, measures (based on information derived from reporting events occurring in prisons or by examining samples of inmates) are suggested for the following three functions of incarceration:

1. To hold inmates securely—protecting the public, exacting a penalty from inmates and maintaining internal security to protect inmates from dangerous offenders, and to protect corrections officers working inside the prison (Measures 1–3);
2. To hold inmates humanely—meeting their needs for adequate housing, medical care, food, and clothing, and providing any other civil rights granted them by the Constitution, legislation, and courts (Measures 4–6);
3. To rehabilitate offenders—so that they do not commit crimes when released (because of a "corrected" attitude, because of the unpleasantness of incarceration, or because of new skills (Measure 7)).

As noted earlier, opinions differ among correctional officials and in society at large as to the relative importance of these functions. Still, corrections agencies may want to monitor aspects of each function. Seven measures are suggested. Additional measurement concepts which a corrections agency could use for a special study or might want to develop for periodic monitoring also are touched on here and outlined in detail in Appendix A. The seven main measures covered are not "diagnostic"—that is, they do not indicate directly what should be done to correct conditions. They are intended to provide officials with a perspective on the overall magnitude of the problems and trends. If values for a measure (for example, escapes or physical assaults by inmates on other inmates) become alarming or show a sudden increase, officials may also want to investigate each incident in detail to determine the root causes and to identify possible corrective action.

TO HOLD INMATES SECURELY

For this objective three basic measures are suggested for annual monitoring:

Measure 1: *Escape rates (annual number of escapes divided by annual average daily population), by level of security*

This measure shows the ability of correctional facilities to contain offenders. The data should be presented by level of security (maximum, medium, minimum) at which the escapee was being held, because the threat to the community of inmate escapes and the efforts made in holding the offenders vary by security

Exhibit 3
ILLUSTRATIVE PRESENTATION OF ESCAPE RATES

1975 Escape Rates from North Carolina Correctional Institutions
by Custody Level

Security Level of Facility	Number of Escapes in 1975	Average Daily Population	Escape Rate per 1,000 Inmate-Years
Minimum	10	149	67.1
Medium	0	561	0
Close	0	493	0
Maximum	1	1,255	0.8
Mixed	34	473	71.9
OVERALL ESCAPE RATE	45	2,931	15.4

Note: This exhibit does not include data from minimum security camps housing approximately 10,000 offenders.
SOURCE: North Carolina Department of Correction, *Statistical Data in Support of the Budget for FY 1975–77 Biennium.*

level. Some states regularly report these data.[1] (See exhibit 3.) Although relatively few escapes occur from maximum- and medium-security levels, the data are useful for comparisons over time and as points of reference for the lower levels of security.

Expressing the value of the measure as an escape rate—the number of escapes divided by the average daily population (ADP) for the whole year in the various levels of security—permits comparisons among facilities and over time, even if the inmate populations change. States with more than one facility at each level of security might want to tally the data by facility. Daily statistics on total-system and total-facility population are probably readily available. Computers will enable officials to obtain ADPs with minimal added effort, but if there is no automated capability, ADPs can be obtained manually by dividing the yearly total of inmate-days by 365 (or 366 in leap years). When a facility has more than one level of security, calculation of ADP will be substantially more complicated, perhaps requiring some type of record sampling, unless daily population statistics are kept on the number at each level of security within the facility.

A corrections agency might want to distinguish between *escapes* (unauthorized leave from a facility where offenders are guarded or physically contained) and *walkaways* or *runaways* (unauthorized leave from a facility or location in the community where offenders are not guarded nor physically contained—perhaps because they are on "trustee" status or on work release). If this distinction is made, to obtain appropriate

rates it may then be necessary to estimate for each facility the ADPs of guarded and unguarded inmates. For example, it might be appropriate to use a variation of the measure such as the annual number of walkaways divided by the annual number of offender-days on work-release status.

Many states have a special procedure for reporting escapes that would provide the data for the number of escapes and level of custody facility needed for this measure. If the population and escape data are stored in an automated data processing system, the measure should be available with virtually no extra effort on the part of the monitoring personnel once appropriate program and data-routing procedures have been established. If such data are not available, the value of this measure can be calculated in a simple, but possibly time-consuming, hand method.

A related measure which might be examined, perhaps as a part of a special study to help interpret escape data, is *percentage of escapees recaptured (or escapees who surrender), by time period since escape.* This measures the performance of corrections and other criminal justice agencies in recapturing offenders, the extent to which the public is "at risk," and when offenders are not recaptured, the extent of failure of corrections to punish offenders. The data for recapture are filed in inmate folders by some states. They might be classified according to recapture within one day, within seven days, within thirty days, or within one year.

---

1. A number of variations exist. For example, California has expressed escapes as the number of felons escaping from guarded perimeters of medium/maximum security institutions per 100 ADP. Alaska has used a measure of the number of escapes, per 10,000 person-days of confinement. Michigan has used the number of escapes and walkaways, as a percentage of average inmate population at the facility.

Measure 2: *Number of crimes against the public ascribed to escapees and to inmates on authorized absence (such as work release), by type of offense*

This measure provides an estimate of the impact on the public of security failures that result in crimes by inmates who either have escaped or are on work release, home visits, or other authorized release programs. Apparently, no agency regularly monitors this impact. From the standpoint of ultimate impact, it would be more meaningful than Measure 1.

The number of crimes actually committed is virtually impossible to determine accurately. Some crimes will not be reported, others will not be attributed to escapees, while still others that are reported will be attributed falsely to escapees. Data regarding either the number of formal charges levied or the number of convictions are useful.

The use of either formal charges or convictions is likely to underestimate substantially the number of crimes, because some offenders escape formal charges by eluding capture and others may not be charged with offenses when seized. The use of formal charges rather than convictions would result in a higher estimate of the number of crimes committed (and probably would include some unjustified charges as well as some actual offenses which do not lead to conviction). But such data would be available without waiting for court actions. In light of the increased reliability of conviction data, some states may prefer to use convictions. (The issue is discussed at greater length under Measures 8 and 9.)

Data on charges and convictions are likely to be contained in case folders of recaptured offenders. Unless the agency keeps a special tally on authorized absentees, screening such persons for either charges or convictions may be more difficult.

It is suggested that crimes be categorized as offenses against property or offenses against persons. Crimes committed to achieve the escape, such as theft or destruction of prison property or attacks on prison officials, would not necessarily be counted as impacts on the public, but they might be counted separately.

Measure 3: *Annual number of incidents of failure of internal security, by type of incident (contraband, unrest, assault on staff, assault on inmates), total, and total divided by ADP*

Holding inmates securely also involves controlling conditions so that the prison is safe for inmates and prison officials. Measure 3 produces information on impacts of internal security conditions. Prison systems frequently document in some way the various failures that occur, and some may record the number of incidents in a year. The only evidence of systematic definition of incident types, recording and collating of incident reports, and periodic summarization of the

data found in this project, however, was in North Carolina. Measure 3 consists of a count of incidents involving contraband; incidents of general prison unrest; physical assault(s) by inmates(s) on prison staff; and physical assault(s) by inmate(s) on other inmate(s).

Exhibit 4 shows an incident/assault report, developed and implemented by the North Carolina Department of Correction as a result of this project, to cover each incident in each facility. The total number of incidents each year at each level of security (and possibly at each facility) would be summarized from the individual reports. The total number and the rates (total number divided by the ADP at each level of security) could be entered on a similar form to display results. A corrections agency might also want to calculate the total number of inmates involved in all of the incidents. Moreover, because security breaches are expected to increase with prison population, particularly when overcrowding occurs, it is important to divide the numbers of incidents by the ADP and present the result along with the total number of incidents. A single incident can be recorded in from one to four of the categories on the reporting form, so a total of the summaries of individual incidents can yield more incidents than actually took place. If officials are concerned about possible multiple counting, they should total the number of reports received as well as the individual incidents.

If incidents stem in part from overcrowding, understaffing, or inadequate facilities, officials may not be able to take immediate steps to improve conditions; but at least the measure could help demonstrate the need for more facilities, enlarged staff, or better classification.

Some issues associated with reports of the various types of incidents are discussed separately below:

Incidents involving contraband, by type, total number, and number divided by ADP

Despite prison security, contraband—particularly drugs, escape equipment, and weapons—inevitably seems to penetrate even the most secure prisons.[2] Because of reports from informants, many prison officials feel knowledgeable about the extent of contraband, especially drugs,[3] in their prisons. But although

---

2. Various items of contraband and a classification method are described by Anthony L. Guenther, "The Forms and Functions of Prison Contraband," in *Crime and Delinquency*.

3. The injection or ingestion of certain types of drugs (opiates, amphetamines, barbiturates) can be detected for periods of twenty-four to forty-eight hours after intake by urinalysis, providing a possible approach for estimating the prevalence of this type of contraband. The North Carolina Department of Correction once attempted such a test on a sample of offenders, but offenders learned through the prison grapevine of the impending examination and ap-

Exhibit 4
ILLUSTRATIVE REPORT FORMAT

North Carolina Department of Correction
INCIDENT/ASSAULT REPORT

DC-418
6/76

To be completed at unit for each incident. If incident belongs to more than one category, check all that apply. Forward to Office of Research and Evaluation within three days of occurrence.

Unit Number _____
Unit Name _____
Custody of Unit _____
Date _____
Area _____

A. *INCIDENT INVOLVING CONTRABAND*—Do not report the mere appearance of small amounts of contraband—only overt incidents arising from the use or discovery of contraband items, or large volume indicating traffic.

Nature of incident
- ☐ Illness—inmate becomes ill as a result of consuming contraband material.
- ☐ Assault—contraband used as weapon. (Report also in Section C and/or D).
- ☐ Escape or Attempt—contraband used as weapon. (Report also—if applicable—in Section B).
- ☐ Large volume discovered, indicating possible trafficking.
- ☐ Other _____

Type of Contraband
- ☐ Drugs
- ☐ Weapons
- ☐ Other _____
  _____
  _____

Seriousness
- ☐ Death
- ☐ Hospitalization—admitted as inpatient.
- ☐ Medical attention required—including outpatient status.
- ☐ No medical attention required.
- ☐ Damage to buildings.
- ☐ Damage to furniture, equipment.

B. *INCIDENT OF UNREST*—Report only the actions of a group of inmates, not those of an individual such as a solitary hunger strike.

Nature of incident
- ☐ Riot
- ☐ Strike
- ☐ Sit-in
- ☐ Mass Escape (3 or more inmates)

Complaint or Cause
- ☐ Correctional Services
- ☐ Correctional facilities
- ☐ Rules and regulations
- ☐ Inmate action or pressures.
- ☐ Other _____
  _____
  _____
  _____

Seriousness
- ____ Number of participants.
- ____ Number Staff injuries.
- ____ Number inmate injuries.
- ☐ Damage to buildings.
- ☐ Damage to furniture, equipment.

C. *PHYSICAL ASSAULT ON STAFF*—Report only instances in which a physical assault occurred or was averted by physical restraint.

Nature of incident
- ☐ Weapon used in assault
- ☐ Unarmed—no weapon used

____ Number of victims

____ Number of assailants

Seriousness
- ☐ Death
- ☐ Hospitalization—admitted as inpatient.
- ☐ Medical attention required—including outpatient status.
- ☐ No medical attention required.

D. *PHYSICAL ASSAULT ON FELLOW INMATES*—Report only instances in which a physical assault occurred or was averted by physical restraint.

Nature of incident
- ☐ Weapon used in assault
- ☐ Unarmed—no weapon used
- ☐ Sexual assault

_____ Number of victims

_____ Number of assailants

Seriousness
- ☐ Death
- ☐ Hospitalization—admitted as inpatient.
- ☐ Medical attention required—including outpatient status.

SOURCE: North Carolina Department of Correction.

---

this information—and more particularly, information about weapons or escape equipment—may be quite useful for ordering shakedowns or for intensifying security, it is difficult to report, and its accuracy and impacts are not obvious.

Much of the contraband will never be detected. Some of it, however, will create *observable* disturbances or conditions when used, such as

- Illnesses and assaults in which inmates or officials receive medical attention because of the use of contraband drugs or weapons. Problems can include drug overdoses, serum hepatitis, wounds from stabs, and bludgeoning.
- Escapes and escape attempts where contraband items (saws, files, ropes, keys, and so forth) are used.
- Prison disturbances incited by alcohol or drugs, or involving weapons.

This evidence of contraband is sometimes noted in various records (such as incident or escape reports) at prison units, but it is seldom classified and tallied for use in performance monitoring. The number of incidents involving contraband will provide a minimum estimate of contraband impacts. The accuracy of the data will be limited because it is difficult to identify causes of disturbances, because some inmates may

withhold reports of attacks or requests for medical assistance for fear of reprisal from other inmates, and because prison officials may be reluctant to report all incidents of inadequate security for fear of being considered negligent.

Guidelines on reporting incidents appear necessary to minimize inaccuracies resulting from differing opinions among prison officials about what to report. A special report format such as that in exhibit 4 could provide guidelines and standardize reporting. The effort required to obtain data for the measure appears to be minimal if some type of special incident reporting system is already in place and if all reports are routed to a central office. If a central reporting system is not established, it might be possible to search prison records (such as incident or escape reports) to identify contraband incidents, but this procedure would be cumbersome and basically inaccurate because, in the absence of any centrally promulgated guideline, officials in the individual facilities might use different criteria.[4]

Incidents of unrest by groups of inmates; total number and number divided by ADP

Internal security can be disrupted by rioting, mass escape attempts, destruction of facilities, mass sit-ins, hunger strikes, arson, extensive vandalism, or any other actions by groups of inmates in violation of prison regulations or requiring some type of force to disband. Incidents often stem more from the way prisoners feel they are being treated (unfair restrictions of privileges, poor food, or unsanitary conditions) than from poor internal security. Thus, although an incident may con-

---

parently foiled the test by refraining from using drugs just before the test. A senior prison official doubted the success of another test on grounds that inmates would learn of it again or those with drugs in their system would refuse to provide a sample. If the sample could be taken during a comprehensive physical exam (as discussed in a later measure), where the purpose of taking the sample was not so obvious, the test might be more successful. This measure is not suggested for regular monitoring, but some prison systems might want to use it as a special test. Because of the costs of urinalysis, corrections officials might prefer to analyze specimens for a random sample of inmates from the whole prison system (perhaps 200 to 300) or only inmates at particular facilities. The cost of analyzing one specimen can vary from two to five dollars, depending primarily on the types of tests being conducted and the number of specimens analyzed. At the time of this research, there were no widely available urine tests to detect the use of marijuana—perhaps the most commonly used illicit drug in prisons.

4. Some prisons may keep records on the number of items of contraband discovered in a prison facility. The number discovered is difficult to interpret and seems unreliable for estimating the total contraband in the facility. Does a high number mean success in removing contraband or a lack of success in keeping it out? The number depends on the thoroughness of the search, the number of searches, the time period between searches, and warning of impending searches. These characteristics appear to keep this concept from being valid enough to be useful for annual monitoring.

stitute a part of inadequate internal security, it may also indicate some other type of problem, and perhaps one beyond the immediate control of officials at the facility. A form such as the one in exhibit 4 provides a way to collect the data. Data from the forms can be tallied to yield the number of inmates involved as well as the total number and type of incidents and possibile causes.

Physical assaults on prison officials; total number and number divided by ADP

Even in the best-maintained security systems, prison officials—especially guards—will still be at some risk and susceptible to assault. Many corrections systems record information on physical assaults (in incident reports, facilities and personnel files, or inmate disciplinary files), so data could be obtained from existing prison records. A reporting format such as the one in exhibit 4 would simplify handling the data and classifying it by type of assault.

It can be difficult to interpret changes. Are they due to different ways of handling inmates by officials? To changes in prison population, staffing levels, or staff training? To different types of inmates? Or to differences in what is viewed as an attack (which should be minimal with the definition provided)? Interpretation of changes can be facilitated if each assault is investigated and the causes and contributing factors identified. Michigan, California, Alaska, and Washington have routinely summarized data on the annual number of assaults or incidents of violence. Michigan, for example, calculates the annual number of assaults as a percentage of average inmate population and employees.

Physical assaults on inmates requiring medical treatment; total and total divided by ADP

Court decrees,[5] humane considerations, the explicit objectives in at least two executive budgets,[6] and Standard 2.4 of the *Corrections* report of NACCJSG, require that, insofar as possible, prisons protect offenders from brutalities inflicted by other inmates.[7]

Measure 3 covers only the most severe incidents of failure to protect inmates. It probably greatly underestimates the total number of assaults, particularly

sexual assaults. Because of the "inmate code" against squealing, many inmates will request assistance only if an injury requires substantial medical treatment, and even in these cases, inmates may not be willing to attribute the injury to assault. Prison officials and medical personnel in particular should be able to attribute more serious injuries (or even deaths) to assaults or to accidents. Probable assault injuries include punctures with sharp instruments, bludgeoning, and multiple bruises and abrasions from an attack of substantial force. Obviously, when assaults are serious enough to be reported, they should be investigated, the causes identified, and corrective actions recommended; but because of staff limitation, some agencies may not be able to investigate each.

The issue of inmate protection is a large one, and the single measure suggested above is not likely to provide all of the information corrections officials want. Although it might be viewed as unreliable, one possible approach to monitoring assaults and other inmate-oriented measures is to survey inmates on internal security. By use of a blind or confidential interviewing process, it might be possible to estimate the failure of protection by the percentage reported being assaulted.[8] Another approach is to interview only inmates being discharged or transferred from the facility. The emphasis in the use of such data should probably be in the *changes* that take place over time, rather than on the absolute values.

Problems concerning the credibility of the responses remain, and unless substantial efforts are made to develop and validate a survey instrument, the usefulness of this approach seems limited. This project did not have the resources to develop and validate an instrument, but such efforts should be undertaken (see further discussion in Appendix A).

Suicides

The corrections agency also might want to report on the *annual number of suicides, attempted suicides, and self-inflicted wounds* as a type of internal security failure. As it probably is more difficult for corrections officials to control or reduce these incidents than any of the previous four, and as such incidents do not reflect inadequate protection from other inmates, Measure 3 does not include suicide, attempted suicides, or self-inflicted wounds. Possible definitions for the degree of severity of such incidents are

1. Suicide—the death is ruled by medical examiner to be self-inflicted; or, substantial suicide at-

5. *Gates* v. *Collier,* 349 F.Supp. 881 (N.D. Miss. 1972), off'd., 510 F.2d 1291 (5th Cir., 1974). *Wayne County Jail Inmates et al.* v. *Wayne County Board of Commissioners, et al.,* 1 Pr.L.Reptr. 5 (Wayne County, Michigan, Cir.Ct. 1971.)

6. The 1975–77 Wisconsin Executive Budget contains an objective of Corrections to "protect offenders from the horrors" of incarceration. The District of Columbia FY 1975 Budget calls for the "safe-keeping" of incarcerated offenders.

7. "Each correctional agency should fulfill the right of offenders to be free from personal abuse . . . by other offenders." NACCJSC, *Corrections,* p. 31.

8. Such a surveying technique, called "randomized responses," has been developed by the Research Triangle Institute in North Carolina.

tempt—inmate probably would have died had prison officials not intervened;

2. Self-inflicted wounds—injuries requiring medical treatment but not an apparent attempt to take life.

This information should be available from inmate files or facility records, but it is probably not summarized routinely, except for suicides, reported by some states in an annual summation of terminations. If this information is to be used, a special reporting format would be necessary. It may be difficult to separate wounds, assaults, and self-inflicted wounds. It seems particularly important to determine the cause of suicides and self-inflicted injuries. Are the classification and screening programs inadequate? Are requests for psychological help being denied?

TO HOLD INMATES HUMANELY

Opinions vary on what constitutes humane treatment. It ranges from meeting basic minimum necessities for survival—food, housing, medical maintenance, and physical protection from assaults—or providing, in addition to these basics, certain esthetic amenities. Prison amenities encompass vocational and educational development and recreational opportunities, comfortable surroundings, comfortable clothing, and home leave or conjugal visits. The extent of humane treatment provided (and the associated degree of monitoring) depends in part on the state's philosophy of treatment and the willingness of the state government and citizens to provide a given level of amenities. This section suggests measures only of what might be considered the basic necessities for survival. If there is vital interest in some of the so-called amenities, they might be examined in a special study, and measures to monitor them could be developed. The three measures suggested for annual monitoring follow.

Measure 4: *Annual number of inmate-days of overcrowding, by facility*

Overcrowding is undesirable. It can cause deterioration of security, health, and internal order. (Although each of these aspects has specific measures discussed elsewhere, a direct measure of overcrowding appears useful.) Overcrowding can occur when more inmates use facilities or participate in rehabilitation programs than the facilities or programs were designed to accommodate. It can occur because of a modification in facilities which reduces capacity or because of a reduction in staff which reduces the level of inmate security and treatment. As prison populations often fluctuate substantially from month to month, corrections agencies that rely on annual average popu-

lation figures in fact may be underestimating their overcrowding problem.[9]

Measure 4 is based on the cumulative amount of any daily overcrowding—specifically, the number of inmates housed in a facility in excess of the number the sleeping quarters were designed to hold. Thus, if a dormitory at a particular facility were designed to accommodate 100 inmates, and 120 slept there one night, the measure of overcrowding would be twenty inmate-days for one day. The total overcrowding would be the annual summation of any daily overcrowding in each of the facilities. As yet no state appears to use this measure.

Overcrowding can be estimated by reviewing a sample of daily prison logs on offender custody. Relatively simple data-processing procedures could be established for daily or weekly calculation of information, especially if the daily population is entered into a computer file. Although the prison population can be obtained accurately, the given or stated capacity figure is often likely to be inaccurate, and a special effort could be required to obtain an accurate estimate of capacity.[10]

Another form of this measure, which provides slightly less information and thus appears less desirable generally, is the number of days per year when inmate population exceeds rated, available capacity. This form of the measure provides information on the frequency of overcrowding, but not on its severity. Values for this form are determined somewhat more easily, especially if hand tabulations have to be made. The value can be determined by reviewing daily population records and tallying each day that the population in a facility exceeds the predetermined capacity figure.

---

9. For example, if during six months of the year the facility operated at 20 percent below capacity and during the other six months at 20 percent above capacity, the annual average population compared with capacity would not show any overcrowding, which would be misleading. In facilities that are almost always heavily overcrowded, the average population is more meaningful.

10. It is beyond the scope of this project to provide guidelines on how to determine the capacity of a facility. Clearly, an accurate determination—considering sleeping, eating, recreational, rehabilitation, and security needs—is important if this measure is to be meaningful. Design-capacity figures probably become inaccurate when the facility is modified, either structurally or by using an area for a purpose other than its designed purpose (e.g., using dormitory space for a vocational-rehabilitation work area). It is more accurate to use currently available capacity rather than designed capacity to reflect overcrowding that occurs when various sections are closed for repairs, etc. Capacity figures frequently quoted by corrections agencies for the most part probably are outdated and overstated. Corrections agencies using this measure should audit periodically the capacity figures used for this measure. They should also determine if bedding or some other need, such as recreational space or even toilet facilities, is the limiting factor.

Exhibit 5
ILLUSTRATIVE SANITATION RATING SCALES

DEPARTMENT OF HUMAN RESOURCES
DIVISION OF HEALTH SERVICES
SCORE SHEET FOR
LOCAL CONFINEMENT FACILITIES

—————————————————— ——————————
Health Department   Demerit Score
                           Classification:

——————————————————
Name of Facility   Approved—————————

——————————————————   Provisional————————
Address of Facility
                           Disapproved———————

——————————————————
Person in charge at time of inspection, and title

	Demerit Points
1. FLOORS: Easily cleanable, in good repair 1; kept clean 2; sloped, impervious, and floor drain, if required 2_	_____
2. WALLS AND CEILINGS: Easily cleanable, in good repair 1; light colored, washable to level of splash 2; kept clean 2	_____
3. LIGHTING AND VENTILATION: Adequate in all areas as required 4; fixtures, equipment in good repair and clean 4; special vents for kitchen, etc., effective and kept clean 4 ___	_____
4. TOILET, HANDWASHING AND BATHING FACILITIES: Toilet, handwashing, bathing facilities adequate, convenient, comply with Building Code 2; fixtures approved, in good repair, and clean 2; lavatory provided in kitchen 2; mixing faucet, soap, towels 1; hot water supply adequate 4	_____
5. WATER SUPPLY: Public supply; private supply (approved, adequate) 6; hot and cold water piped to points of use 4	_____
6. DRINKING WATER FACILITIES: Fountains or individual drinking cups provided 4; fountains of approved type, regulated, clean 2; multi-use cups easily cleanable construction, cleaned and sanitized daily and before use by succeeding persons 2 _	_____
7. LIQUID WASTES: Sewage and other liquid wastes disposed of by approved method 6; on-site disposal system properly operated, no nuisance 2	_____

Score Sheet

	Demerit Points
8. SOLID WASTES: Garbage in standard containers, properly covered and stored; can cleaning facilities; containers, storage room clean 4; dry rubbish in suitable receptacles, properly stored and disposed of 2 _____	_____
9. VERMIN CONTROL, PREMISES: Outside openings effectively screened or otherwise protected against entrance of flies, etc., or flies absent 4; effective control of rodents or other vermin 4; pesticides properly used and stored 2; premises clean and free of vermin harborages and breeding areas 2	_____
10. STORAGE: Adequate facilities provided for storage of necessary janitorial supplies and equipment, mattresses, and linen 2; mop receptors or sinks provided and used 2; facilities clean 2	_____
11. MATTRESSES—MATTRESS COVERS—BED LINEN: Furniture, bunks, mattresses, etc., clean and in good repair 4; linen clean and in good repair, properly stored and handled 2; soiled linen properly handled and stored 1	
12. FOOD SERVICE UTENSILS AND EQUIPMENT: Easily cleanable construction, in good repair, kept clean 4; food-contact surfaces accessible for cleaning, non-toxic, etc., free of open crevices 4	_____
13. CLEANING AND SANITIZING OF FOOD SERVICE UTENSILS AND EQUIPMENT: Multi-use eating and drinking utensils clean and sanitized after each use 4; cooking and storage utensils cleaned after each use 2; facilities for washing and sanitizing approved, adequate, properly maintained (booster heater when necessary) 4; substances containing poisonous material not used for cleaning or polishing eating or cooking utensils 6; cloths used in kitchen clean 2	_____
14. STORAGE AND HANDLING OF FOOD SERVICE UTENSILS AND EQUIPMENT: Sanitized utensils stored in clean place 2; cooking and storage utensils properly stored and handled 2; no contamination of food-contact	

(14 Cont'd)	Demerit Points		Dermit Points

surfaces of equipment 2; single-service utensils properly stored and handled 2 _____   _____

15. FOOD SUPPLIES AND PROTECTION: Supplies: All food clean, wholesome, no spoilage; potentially hazardous foods from approved sources, properly identified 6; Grade A pasteurized fluid milk for drinking, dry milk reconstituted for cooking only 4; meals from approved sources if other than jail kitchen 6; single-service utensils used by alternate source 4; Protection: Adequate during storage, preparation, display, service, and transportation; potentially hazardous food below 45°F. or above 140°F. 4; storage facilities ade-

quate, all refrigerators with thermo-meters 2; pork stuffings, etc., thoroughly cooked; meat and poultry salad, potato salad, etc., handled as required; no re-serving 4; adequate facilities for cold and hot food storage 2; food containers stored above floor and protected from splash and other contamination 2; no live animals or fowl 2 _____   _____

16. FOOD SERVICE WORKERS: Clean coats, caps, or special dress 2; clean hands and work habits 4 _____   _____

DATE_____ SIGNED _____ AGENT
Department of Human Resources

SOURCE: North Carolina Department of Human Resources, Division of Health Services, Sanitary Engineering Section, ''Rules and Regulations Governing the Sanitation of Local Confinement Facilities.''

Measure 5: *Rating of sanitation conditions in prison facilities*

Sanitation conditions in correctional facilites can have an important effect on the health and well-being of inmates. The National Advisory Commission on Criminal Justice Standards and Goals has suggested:

Each correctional agency should immediately examine and take action to fulfill the right of each person in its custody to a healthful place in which to live.[11]

Corrections or health officials in many states inspect prisons for sanitation, and sometimes improvements are made as a result of these inspections. An American Bar Association survey published in 1974 identified fifteen states with laws providing for minimum standards.[12] Twenty-four of the states surveyed in 1976 as part of this project indicated that they inspect prison facilities, but the scope of these inspections varies. In some states, there were no established criteria—only the judgments of the inspectors on what to look for.

The limited scope of this project precluded an extensive review of the legislation and guidelines various states use for inspections. A substantial effort to review the guidelines now existing, to develop additional procedures, and to put together and test a comprehensive inspection package for feasibility and reliability could develop a procedure useful to many states.

A rating scale could be developed on the basis of quantitative ratings of conditions most likely to affect the health of inmates.[13] Emphasis would be placed on inspections of food-handling, preparation, and storage practices; vermin control; bathing, drinking, and toilet facilities; liquid and solid waste disposal; and fire hazards. Exhibit 5 shows a rating form developed by North Carolina Health Department inspectors giving the number of demerits for failure to meet specific sanitary conditions. Exhibit 6 illustrates one method of displaying the rating data.[14]

State health department personnel generally already have the technical knowledge required to establish prison health and sanitation criteria, including access to existing health and sanitation codes and

---

11. NACCJSG, *Corrections*, p. 34.

12. *Survey and Handbook on State Standards and Inspection Legislation for Jails and Juvenile Detention Facilities.* Prepared by the Statewide Jail Standards and Inspection Systems Project, American Bar Association Commission on Correctional Facilities and Services.

13. This measure indicates the extent of meeting ''standards'' rather than the impact of conditions on offenders, which is somewhat at variance with the project emphasis of developing ''impact'' or ''outcome'' measures. Yet it still seems useful if the standards relate to conditions known to affect or likely to lead to deterioration in physical and mental health or if they relate to conditions contrary to public expectations for sanitation.

14. A proxy measure of the impact of unsanitary conditions would be the number of inmates, or the number of inmate-days, in facilities which were not in compliance with sanitation standards. A problem with this measure is that all of the inmates in a facility might not be affected by the noncompliance; nonfunctioning of toilets on one tier of a prison does not mean that all inmates in the facility suffer.

Exhibit 6
ILLUSTRATIVE SANITATION RATING DATA

Demerits Received During Sanitation
Inspection in 1976

Name of Prison Facility	Demerits Received
Central Prison	36
Caledonia Correctional Institution	19
Odom Correctional Institution	20
North Carolina Correctional Center for Women	40
Blanch Correctional Institution	32

SOURCE: North Carolina Department of Correction, *Statistical Data in Support of the Budget for FY 1975–77 Biennium.*

inspection procedures for rating conditions in non-penal institutions. Hence, these persons are likely to be the appropriate ones to establish inspection procedures: the conditions to be examined, rating scales and demerits, criteria for making ratings, and reporting formats. After the inspection system has been established, inspection of a facility probably can be conducted with no more than one person-day of inspection staff time (plus travel). Each facility should be inspected at least once a year. If many of the deficiencies identified can be corrected with relatively little or no capital outlay and with little delay (for example, better food-handling and preparation practices or more thorough cleaning of toilet areas), inspections might be conducted quarterly—preferably unannounced.

State corrections agencies will find it hard to bring some facilities into compliance because of overcrowding, antiquated facilities, and shortages of funds needed for structural improvements or new equipment. Nevertheless, the status of conditions should be monitored. The rating program will provide data to help the agency justify its needs for funding. Many items, particularly those relating to food-handling practices and to cleanliness of the facilities, can be remedied with little or no additional expenditure. It may be useful to have two rating scales, one relating to structural and other conditions over which the warden has little control without additional money and a second, relating to more controllable conditions.

Measure 6: *Percentage of inmates with unmet health needs*

"Each correctional agency should take immediate steps to fulfill the right of offenders to medical care. This should include services guaranteeing physical, mental, and social well-being, as well as treatment for specific diseases or infirmities."[15] This standard from the NACCJSG *Corrections* volume, plus numerous court decisions, stated objectives of many corrections agencies, and basic humanitarian considerations justify the provision of medical services and some monitoring of their quality, particularly for persons who have been incarcerated for relatively long periods of time and whose health has had time to deteriorate.[16]

Many offenders not only have physical problems when entering, but also develop physical and mental illnesses during incarceration.[17] A health examination at entrance, treatment for any infirmities at that time, and treatment when requested by inmates do not guarantee the continuance of good health for persons with long-term incarceration. During incarceration they can develop illnesses which, though debilitating, are unaccompanied by acute pain that might prompt medical attention or even requests for attention. They also can suffer from receiving insufficient care for identified health problems.

Exhibit 7 shows the problems uncovered among a randomly selected sample of 458 inmates in the Michigan Correctional System.[18] About 180 health problems requiring referral for additional treatment were found for every 100 inmates examined.[19] Compared to the national average of the same age group, offenders tended to be underweight, to have higher than normal incidence of genito-urinary tract infections (82 percent of female inmates had problems), and to have abnormally low white blood-cell counts, a high number of abnormal hematocrits and lower mean hematocrit levels (suggesting malnutrition), and, among black inmates, a high rate of liver problems. Hypertension, trauma, seizures, epilepsy, infectious hepatitis, gastroenteritis, upper respiratory infections, neurosis and acute depression, severe tooth gum problems, and

---

15. NACCJSG, *Corrections*, p. 36.

16. Some of the justifications are quoted in NACCJSG, *Corrections*, p. 37. Others include *Battle* v. *Anderson*, 376 F.Supp. 402 (E.D. Okla., May 30, 1975) and *Newman* v. *Alabama*, 349 F.Supp. 278 (M.C. Ala. 1972).

17. Two publications which discuss the prison health issue are *Medical and Health Care in Jails, Prisons, and Other Correctional Facilities,* prepared by the American Bar Association in conjunction with the American Medical Association, and Seth B. Goldsmith, *Prison Health.* Goldsmith presents some statistics on health conditions of persons at intake.

18. Office of Health and Medical Affairs, *Key to Health for a Padlocked Society.* See in particular Appendix F, "Methodology for a Clinical Assessment Report."

19. Statistics were not reported on the percentage of the sample with at least one problem requiring referral. At a minimum, it was 33.4 percent (based only on those with genito-urinary tract problems).

venereal diseases are other specific illnesses believed to occur relatively frequently in prisons.[20]

Although many corrections agencies give health examinations to offenders when they enter prison,[21] apparently no state corrections agency routinely monitors the health of incarcerated offenders by regularly examining random samples of inmates either during incarceration or upon discharge. Only Michigan has conducted an ad hoc evaluation of inmate health (but there have been examinations of prison health care procedures elsewhere). The procedures and the basic measure used in Michigan—the percentage needing referral for additional treatment—appear appropriate for other states.[22]

Medical examination of a representative cross section of inmates appears to be the most thorough approach to determining whether additional attention needs to be directed toward providing health care. If at intake the corrections system provides what is felt to be comprehensive examination with adequate referral services, the sample might be drawn only from inmates incarcerated long enough for deterioration in health to be likely to set in (perhaps a minimum of six to twelve months). A comparison of health conditions of inmates with those of nonincarcerated persons with the same general characteristics, as done in the Michigan study, appears worthwhile to determine if health care (or healthy conditions) of inmates is significantly worse than for the public at large.[23]

The costs of health measurement depend chiefly

---

20. See Mary Sue Protzel, "Nursing Behind Bars," *American Journal of Nursing,* 27(3): 505–508, March 1972; "Treatment Behind Bars," 102:35–36, July 9, 1973; Seth B. Goldsmith, "The Status of Prison Health Care: A Review of the Literature," *Public Health Reporter,* 89(6): 569–575, Nov./Dec. 1974; and Bery Engebretsen and J. W. Olson, "Primary Care in a Penal Institution: A Study of Health Care Problems Encountered," *Medical Care,* 19(9): 775–781, September 1975.

21. Kentucky conducted an extensive assessment of its correctional health system, but it concentrated on the structure and process of delivery care rather than on inmate health. See Task Force on Prison and Jail Health, *The Captive Patient: Prison Care in Kentucky.*

22. The procedures and tests conducted are discussed in a report prepared by the Office of Health and Medical Affairs, *Key to Health for a Padlocked Society: A Technical Supplement.*

23. There are a number of severe problems in delivering health care services in a penal institution. The environment itself creates certain health problems. The inmates may attempt to abuse the medical delivery system in order to pass the time, to avoid working, to get out of a cell, to seek tranquilizations for nonmedical reasons, or to be disruptive. Health care often is hampered by its low legislative priority, the limited funds for medical services, and the difficulties in filling staff positions. Many of the problems are discussed by Robert L. Brutsche (Assistant Surgeon General, U.S.P.H.S. and Medical Director, U.S. Bureau of Prisons) in "Problems in Health Care Delivery in Penal Institutions," *New York State Journal of Medicine,* June 1975, pp. 1082–1084.

Exhibit 7

MEDICAL EXAMINATION OF 458* RANDOMLY SELECTED INMATES

Percentage of Sample Referred for Additional Treatment by Sex and Body System

Body System	Men (total examined = 411)		Women (total examined = 45)	
	% Not Referred	% Referred	% Not Referred	% Referred
Vision	80.0	20.0	55.6	44.4
Hearing	78.8	21.2	88.9	11.1
Obesity	92.7	7.3	86.7	13.3
Hypertension	79.6	20.4	75.6	24.4
Liver	81.8	18.2	86.7	13.3
Genito-urinary	74.5	25.5	17.8	82.2
Lungs	90.0	10.0	91.1	8.9
Sickle cell	93.9	6.1	91.1	8.9
Ears, nose, throat	98.5	1.5	97.8	2.2
Breasts	99.8	0.2	95.6	4.4
Cardiac, circulation	87.6	12.4	73.3	26.7
Abdomen	97.3	2.7	100.0	0.0
Back	99.0	1.0	97.8	2.2
Rectal	97.1	2.9	97.8	2.2
Skin	94.2	5.8	95.6	4.4
Neurological	96.6	3.4	97.8	2.2
Extremities	92.5	7.5	95.6	4.4
Blood	85.4	14.6	84.4	15.6
Diabetes	96.1	3.9	100.0	0.0
Thyroid	98.3	1.7	93.3	6.7

* Missing observations: 2

SOURCE: Office of Health and Medical Affairs, *Key to Health for a Padlocked Society;* p. 232

---

on the number of tests run on each inmate and of course, on sample size. Assuming the use of no state medical personnel or donated services, one could expect a survey like that done in Michigan to cost about $200 per inmate (1976 prices).[24] This estimate would provide for a series of tests covering the body system components identified in exhibit 7. The costs could be much reduced by eliminating relatively expensive psychological tests, EKG's and dental examinations, although there are likely to be high incidence rates or needs for referrals in these areas. Using state laboratories to analyze blood and urine samples could reduce costs; so the testing might be achieved at a cost of approximately $100 per inmate. If doctors from the

24. This figure is based on a rough estimate by Jeffrey Taylor who was the Assistant Director for Clinical Assessment in the Michigan study.

state department of health are used, or if doctors donate their services, expenditures could be reduced further. If resources permit, it might be desirable to use only medical personnel not regularly employed by the corrections agency in order to minimize charges of nonobjectivity. If one judges by the Michigan experience, about six to nine person-months of staff effort would be required to plan and schedule the examinations of 500 inmates and to-analyze and interpret the data.

The proportion of inmates to be examined will probably depend on the number of facilities and the desired use of the data. An examination of a sample of 100 to 200 inmates, randomly selected from all inmates throughout the system, would give a general view of health. As the quality of health usually varies substantially among facilities (depending on the availability of medical care; the age, race, and sex of inmates; and the upkeep of the facility), larger corrections agencies might want to examine perhaps 100 inmates from each institution and each major category of offender.

It seems helpful to distinguish between inmates with "major" and "minor" unmet health needs. "Minor" could be defined as a problem that is not receiving treatment, but which, even if not treated, is not likely to result in prolonged debilitation, permanent impairment, hospitalization, or acute discomfort for the person affected, nor is it likely to have any "non-minor" effects on other inmates. A "major" need would be any other problem. The exact definition seems less important than the consistency with which it is applied in order that comparisons will be meaningful. State health officials probably should be consulted to help establish the definitions to be applied.

Any state undertaking such an examination would need to determine carefully the feasibility of the specific examinations to be used, and costs. There is a great deal of literature on health care evaluation in nonpenal settings. It should be reviewed and particular attention paid to such potentially troublesome aspects for the corrections area as

- Reliability. If this sample examination approach is used, could two or more physicians making independent examinations of the same offender arrive at similar diagnoses? How reliable are the lab tests of blood and urine samples?
- Public credibility. Would the examinations have to be made by physicians who are not associated with the corrections agency?
- Professional credibility. Would such an approach be recognized as credible by prison health officials as well as by state health associations and the state medical community?
- Validity. Would examination of relatively few

types of conditions be sufficient to identify most of the severe health care problems (say 75 percent of those suffered by inmates)?

Other Possible Measures

Some additional health measures which are not so comprehensive as Measure 6 but which some agencies might want to monitor follow:

Inmate deaths, by cause of death, total, and total divided by ADP

This number is expected to be very low, yet it might indicate a few extreme examples of inadequacies in the prison health system. The data should be readily available, and the information on cause of death should be reliable if each death is investigated by an independent medical examiner. The examination should try to determine if inadequate health care or some other aspect of incarceration contributed to the death. The number of such "prison-related" deaths would be particularly meaningful. It might be compared with mortality rates for nonincarcerated persons to see if persons in prison die at a higher rate. This would not, however, necessarily indicate that prisons provide poor medical care; inmates might generally be in poorer health when first incarcerated than the rest of the population.

Incidence rate of reported illnesses endemic to an institutional environment, by facility

Persons living in close contact with each other in institutions are apt to have higher incidence rates of certain infectious diseases than the population at large. A combined measure of effects of incarceration on the health of offenders, the quality of preventive health care, and possibly of sanitary conditions and crowdedness, is the incidence (i.e., number of illnesses reported in a year divided by ADP) of contagious diseases such as infectious mononucleosis and respiratory ailments (including adenovirus and atypical pneumonia). It is not clear to what extent these illnesses are controllable or preventable by medical care. Thus, the rate might indicate more the impact of incarceration rather than the quality of health care; but regardless of the cause, it is an important impact. These are serious, debilitating illnesses for which inmates would seem likely to request and receive medical diagnoses and treatment. The rates should probably be presented only for the one or two illnesses that occur most often. The occurrence of these illnesses is too sporadic for any sample of inmates examined in Measure 6 to generate reliable statistics. To facilitate comparisons, it

MONITORING THE IMPACTS OF PRISON AND PAROLE SERVICES

might be useful to present incidence rates for the entire prison population.[25]

Percentage of inmates with unmet dental health needs

Many corrections systems provide dental care to inmates who request or are willing to receive it. The Michigan health study found that all of the women and 96 percent of the men in the sample of 458 incarcerated offenders needed dental services other than teeth cleaning. No state correction agency appears to monitor routinely this aspect of health. Data for this measure could be obtained by examining a sample of offenders —possibly the same sample examined for Measure 6. The primary cause of unmet dental needs might be the reluctance of inmates to seek dental care rather than the inadequacies of oral health delivery. If such a measure is used, the need might be classified by severity: ''requires major care'' (more than ''y'' extractions, bridgework, ''x'' or more fillings, etc.); ''requires no care or only minor care'' (''y'' or fewer extractions, cleaning, ''x'' or fewer fillings).

Annual number of lost-time, job-related injuries per 1,000,000 person-hours assigned; annual number of person-hours lost to injury per 1,000,000 hours assigned

Prison industries can be dangerous, especially those involving the use of heavy equipment for metal handling or printing or those involving toxic fumes from sign making and painting. These two measures, using data ordinarily available, could enable corrections officials to monitor the safety of prison industries. It might be useful to categorize the injuries by severity: permanent impairment, temporary impairment with overnight hospitalization or inability to work for more than two days, injury not requiring overnight hospitalization or more than two days off work. But estimating safety based on person-hours lost may prove misleading as some inmates may attempt to be transferred to hospital or other facilities ''just for a change in scenery.'' This is just one measure of the occupational health and safety of prison enterprises. A thorough examination would look at conditions and impacts. But for annual monitoring pur-

poses, a measure such as the one presented here might be sufficient.

TO REHABILITATE INMATES DURING INCARCERATION— CHANGES IN ATTITUDE

Rehabilitation is measured most directly by the behavior of offenders after they are released into the community, as discussed in the next chapter. This section presents intermediate indicators of rehabilitation based on inmate performance while incarcerated. Though they are less satisfying than the in-community ones and their validity for predicting in-community performance has not been well established, they are obtained relatively easily and quickly. Only one indicator is tentatively suggested for periodic monitoring, but others that states might want to consider are mentioned. A research effort spread over several years (or alternatively, an extensive analysis of existing records) would seem to be required to validate these intermediate measures in terms of performance of offenders after they are released.

Measure 7: *Percentages of inmates with substantial improvement-degradation in attitude associated with criminal or social behavior based on psychological test scales administered at intake and at release; numbers of scales showing significant improvement-degradation*

The rigors of incarceration, as well as ''postive'' rehabilitation efforts, are intended in part to change the attitudes and outlooks of incarcerated offenders so that they have more socially acceptable behavior when released to the community and commit no further crimes.

The suggested approach to measuring changes is to administer attitude tests at intake and then again at release (to all inmates or to a statistically random sample) to determine the direction, extent, and types of changes. The Minnesota Multiphasic Personality Inventory (MMPI) is a multidimensional measuring instrument, familiar to many corrections agencies, which can be used to determine change. Some corrections agencies routinely administer the MMPI on intake to all inmates who have an educational achievement level of at least fourth or fifth grade. The North Carolina Department of Correction administers the test to all incoming inmates with at least a fourth-grade achievement level, and for most offenders, scores it on

_____

25. An attempt was made to collect incidence rate data by going through infirmary records in a medium-size facility (population of about 450 minimum-security inmates). The record keeping was so unstructured that determining incidence rates this way did not seem practical. However, in facilities with a resident medical staff and a systematized record keeping system in which illnesses are summarized periodically, it should be possible to obtain values for this measure. They might not fully indicate health status, but they could indicate changes in health status over time.

Exhibit 8
MMPI SCALES

A. Basic MMPI Scales

L	
F	Validity Test Scales
K	
Hs	Bodily function
D	Worry, discouragement, self-esteem, general outlook
Hy	Somatic complaints and emotional or interpersonal difficulty
Pd	Social adjustment
Mf	Masculinity-femininity
Pa	Sensitivity
Pt	Anxiety
Sc	Alienation
Ma	Egotism, expansiveness

B. Prison Classification Inventory Scales

Ec	Prison escape
Ap	Prison adjustment
PAV	Parole violation
Hsx	Homosexual
A	Anxiety
R	Repression and denial
Dc&i	Defective control and inhibition
SD	Sensorimotor disassociation

SOURCE: J. H. Panton, *Interpretive Handbook for the MMPI in Correctional Classification and Diagnostic Services.* This report provides citations to document the various scales and discusses the development and validation of the scales and the specific items included.

---

a number of scales relating to criminality and antisocial behavior as well as on the basic MMPI scales generally used. The scales and overall references for the development and validation of these scales are shown in exhibit 8. The California Psychological Inventory and the 16 Personality Factor test also are used by some state corrections agencies.

Changes in the scores of individual inmates would be examined to determine the percentage of those with apparently significant improvements, and those with apparently significant worsening. Criteria for determining "significance" would need to be established by testing experts. It is desirable to categorize the sample into perhaps two to four groups according to scores at intake so that the amount of change can be related to inmates' condition at intake. It can be argued that the "poorer" the attitudes at intake, the harder it is to make improvements; or, conversely, the "poorer" the attitudes at intake, the more room there is for improvement. Either way, it seems useful for officials to be able to identify the amount of success in making improvements for the various types of incoming inmates.

Another way to indicate change is to calculate the *average* scores on each scale for the whole sample at intake and again at release and then compare the differences. The resulting measure could be expressed as "the number of test scales showing significant improvement, or significant degradation." This measure has the disadvantage that averages can conceal significant changes in individuals. For example, if half the sample improved by a certain amount, and half degraded by that same amount, the averages would indicate no change. But the average scores provide an aggregate measure of condition levels on the individual scales. Statistical significance could be determined by a relatively simple test, so use of this second method would not require the expert judgment needed by the first. However, expert judgment might be required to interpret the meaning or importance of any statistically significant changes.

In the survey of research and evaluation offices for this project, no state corrections agency was found to administer regularly any of these psychological examinations to all inmates or a sample of inmates both at intake and at release and then to compare the pretest and posttest data to measure changes occurring during incarceration.[26]

At the time this report was prepared, a pre/post MMPI test on a sample of inmates being released from incarceration in North Carolina was being developed for application late in 1976. A randomly selected sample of approximately 130 offenders who were about to be released unconditionally or onto parole and who had taken an MMPI test at intake (and whose L, F, and K Scales showed the test results to be valid [e.g., consistent] are to be administered a second MMPI test. The average scores for each of the basic scales and the special criminality scales which apply to behavior in the community (probably all but the Ec and Ap scales) are to be calculated for the entire group. There will be two sets of average scores: one of

---

26. Some states give MMPI tests to certain individuals prior to release on a special request basis (such as a request from the Parole Board or for evaluation of a specific program). The Arkansas Department of Corrections was the only agency found to administer the MMPI twice to all inmates capable of taking it—on entering correctional custody and then three months later, or at release to parole, or at some time during parole. The scores are computed only for the basic MMPI scales, which do not especially relate to criminal attitudes or likely criminal activity. (The scales are subsets of the total of approximately 500 questions.) There have not been any summary comparisons of groups of offenders to determine what, if any, changes have taken place. The department is automating its data files and hopes to be able to make such calculations beginning in 1977. The Utah Department of Corrections has administered the Bi-Polar Personality Inventory on a pre/post basis to one set of offenders being released from incarceration, but it has not instituted the testing on a regular basis.

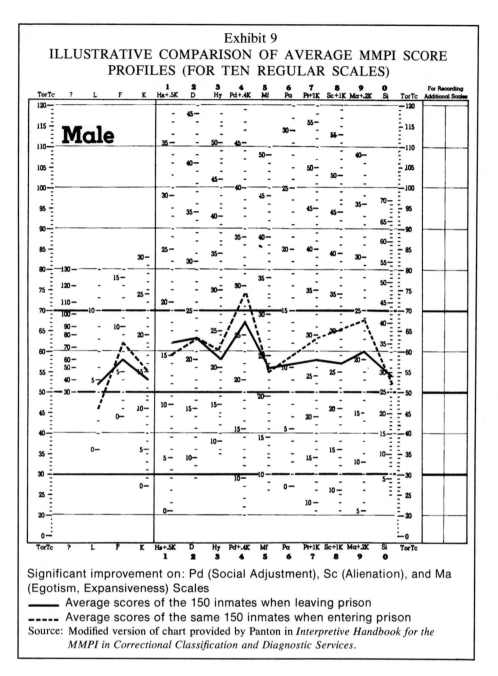

Exhibit 9
ILLUSTRATIVE COMPARISON OF AVERAGE MMPI SCORE PROFILES (FOR TEN REGULAR SCALES)

Male

Significant improvement on: Pd (Social Adjustment), Sc (Alienation), and Ma (Egotism, Expansiveness) Scales

—————— Average scores of the 150 inmates when leaving prison

- - - - - - Average scores of the same 150 inmates when entering prison

Source: Modified version of chart provided by Panton in *Interpretive Handbook for the MMPI in Correctional Classification and Diagnostic Services.*

the scores on intake, calculated from their tests when they entered, the other of the scores when leaving. The preincarceration and postincarceration scores for each scale are to be plotted (similarly to those shown in exhibit 9). Comparisons then should determine if there are significant differences in scores—improvements or degradations—between intake and discharge. Other scoring can be conducted, such as percentage of inmates with substantial improvement/degradation in "x" or more scales.

The central issue is the validity of the scores as indicators of change in behavior. Each of the scales has been documented and validated with one or more groups of persons, but will the scale predict behavior

for prison inmates?[27] The measure should be viewed as tentative until enough experience is obtained to relate recidivism or other measures of community adjustment to the MMPI scores, in order to determine whether the scales predict problems, or lack of them, in postincarceration adjustment in a substantial percentage (70 to 80 percent) of the cases.

---

27. Dahlstrom, Walsh, and Dahlstrom have written the basic text for the MMPI, *An MMPI Handbook*. J. H. Panton identifies a number of scales appropriate for corrections and provides a bibliography for those scales in *Interpretive Handbook for the MMPI in Correctional Classification and Diagnostic Services.*

Other Possible In-Prison Rehabilitation Measures

There have been a number of evaluations of special prison programs for vocational and educational rehabilitation.[28] Arkansas, California, Arizona, Connecticut, Michigan and probably a few other states routinely conduct pretesting and posttesting to determine the educational progress of inmates. Some states already report annually on such aspects as the number of GED (high school equivalency certificates) awarded, the number of offenders completing vocational rehabilitation courses, and the number placed in jobs. At least two states report the amount of offenders' earnings on work-release programs. Measures of education or vocational education achievement while in prison have not been stressed here, primarily because of a lack of information relating such achievement to behavior after release. However, a state corrections agency might view such measures as important intermediate yardsticks of performance and decide to monitor them.

Measures indicating the extent of conformity with prison rules are proposed occasionally. Such measures have not been emphasized here because of the issue of validity; controversy surrounds the question of whether the in-prison behavior indicated by these measures is related to inmates' subsequent behavior on release. In the course of this study, the adage "the best-behaved inmates are the best criminals" was frequently quoted to researchers. As with the psychological test scores, validation could be tested only by examining in-prison performance against subsequent behavior. Two versions of in-prison "good conduct" measures follow:

Percentage of eligible inmates with promotions for good conduct; percentage of inmates demoted for poor conduct in a demotable status

Some corrections systems (including North Carolina's) have a promotion-demotion system, whereby exemplary behavior and adjustment can be rewarded by promotion to or maintenance in an honor grade entitling the offender to certain privileges, possible transfer to a lower level of security, trustee status, a better prison job, or work release. Promotion is based sometimes on a review of behavior after a set period in grade, using established criteria. Unacceptable behavior can be punished by demotion, loss of honor status, or transfer to a higher level of security. Values of the measures can be influenced not only by offender reha-

bilitation or progress but also by space to promote offenders to other facilities, by changes in the level of internal discipline, by criteria used to classify offenders, or by types of inmates. (For example, corrections officials may be reluctant or unwilling to promote inmates to a level at which they can go on work release automatically if the public is still appalled by their offenses.) These factors significantly reduce the validity of the measure. The data on promotions and demotions should be readily available, but the number eligible for promotion—for example, meeting certain time-in-grade requirements—may be harder to obtain.

The annual number of disciplinary actions divided by ADP

This indicator of rehabilitation is very crude, yet, according to Douglas Lipton and his associates, it is frequently used as a measure of institutional adjustment.[29] The number will be affected not only by the actions of the inmates—the aspect of primary concern—but also by the strictness or leniency of individual officials in disciplining inmates, variations in general level of discipline among facilities, and changes in rules or disciplinary philosophies by correctional personnel. The meaning of changes in numbers can be difficult to interpret and an accurate determination of conditions appears impossible.[30] Still, the number of disciplinary actions is readily available, and some corrections agencies might consider it a useful indicator of conditions.[31] Disciplinary problems can be categorized by type of problem or by the severity of punishment. A possible scale follows:[32]

- *Incident of Severe Punishment:* indicated by transfer to another institution for disciplinary reasons or to a higher level of security, seclusion, or solitary confinement in a separate cell.
- *Incident of Moderate Punishment*—Segregation:

---

28. See Lipton, Martinson, and Wilks, *The Effectiveness of Correctional Treatment,* Chapters 3 and 4, for some measures that have been used.

29. Lipton, Martinson, and Wilks, *The Effectiveness of Correctional Treatment.* Chapter 2 shows this measure to be frequently utilized to indicate institutional adjustment.

30. An analogy, pointing out the weaknesses of this type of measure, is to use the number of speeding violations issued to try to determine the number of speeding violations actually occurring. The number is heavily dependent on the amount of effort to catch violators and on the rules set up to define a violation.

31. An alternate measure is the number of incidents of violations. North Carolina Department of Correction officials did not want to use this measure because they specifically encourage prison guards to issue verbal reprimands—of which no records are made—for minor offenses. They feel, as may corrections officials in other states, that measuring the number of incidents would require documenting each and would weaken the system of verbal reprimands.

32. This scale is based on one used by Alfred Blumstein and Jacqueline Cohen, "An Evaluation of a College-level Program in a Maximum Security Prison," p. 70.

indicated by being locked in own cell, segregated for administrative or punitive reasons in another part of the prison, or loss of privileges for twenty-four hours or more.

- *Incident of Mild Punishment:* indicated by reprimand; warning; or probation; loss of commissary, entertainment, or recreation privileges for less than twenty-four hours;[33] or job transfer.

Other Measurements

Other measurements have been used, particularly in evaluations of individual programs, which might be of interest for special studies but which are not recommended as a part of this basic monitoring system. Many can be classified as measures of institutional adjustments; Lipton summarized a number of these.[34]

Two interview approaches which have been developed and used to report on various aspects of prison functioning and environment are the Correctional Institutions Environment Scale (CIES)[35] and a scale developed by Walter C. Reckless and others.[36] Both involve interviews with offenders and with prison officials. As no behavioral evidence of validity was found, their use in a "practical monitoring system" is not stressed. If their validity is established, however, they could be used in developing an instrument for surveying inmates with regard to prison conditions.

33. This is consistent with the definition of minor rules violations of Standard 2.12 of the NACCJSG, *Corrections*.

34. Lipton, Martinson, and Wilks, *The Effectiveness of Correctional Treatment*, pp. 299–333.

35. CIES is described by Ernest Wenk and Rudolph Moos in "Social Climates in Prison: An Attempt to Conceptualize and Measure Environmental Factors in Total Institutions," *Journal of Research in Crime and Delinquency*, 9(2): 134–148, July 1972. See also, Ernest Wenk and Colin Frank, "Some Progress in the Evaluation of Institutional Programs," *Federal Probation*, 39(3), September 1973.

36. Three publications discuss the scale Reckless developed with others: Thomas G. Enyon, Harry E. Allen, Walter C. Reckless, "Measuring Impact of a Juvenile Correctional Institution by Perceptions of Inmates and Staff," *Journal of Research in Crime and Delinquency*, 8(1), January 1971; K. L. Sindwani and Walter C. Reckless, "Prisoners' Perceptions of the Impact of Institutional Stay," *Criminology*, vol. 10, no. 4, February 1974; and Stuart J. Miller and Simon Dinitz, "Measuring Institutional Impact—A Follow-Up," *Criminology* vol. 11, no. 3, November 1973.

CHAPTER III

MEASURES FOR MONITORING OFFENDER REHABILITATION IN THE COMMUNITY

Chapter II discussed measures associated with incarceration and the ability of corrections to hold offenders securely and humanely. Except for Measure 7 (Attitudes) and possibly Measure 2 (Offenses by Escapees), these are all measures of conditions over which the corrections agency can exert a relatively high degree of influence or control (although more funds, facilities, or staff might be needed to achieve the quality desired). This chapter suggests measures of important aspects of offender performance over which the corrections agency probably has much less control. Although some object considerably to using rehabilitation performance as a measure of corrections effectiveness, the authors feel strongly that such performance should be measured, if only to indicate the prison system's difficulties at rehabilitation. Some measurement options are suggested here.

Typically, at least 95 percent of the persons incarcerated eventually will be released to the community. Substantial resources are provided to help achieve rehabilitation in prison, as well as for parole services. Obviously, a major concern to everyone is what happens to offenders when they return to the community. Many corrections agencies and state legislatures will feel that rehabilitation is an appropriate task for corrections. In such states, any system monitoring corrections performance needs to consider the post-incarceration, in-community aspects of offender activities.

Probably the most widely accepted indicator of rehabilitation is the extent of continued criminal activity. Measures 8, 9, and 10 focus on this behavior. Yet current measurement techniques have major deficiencies. Because no apprehension is made for most crimes, conviction and arrest rates—traditional measures of continued criminal activity—accounts generally for less than 20 percent of the total offenses actually committed. Thus the measures are of "known" arrests or "known" convictions, which greatly underestimate the number of offenses committed.

The correlation between the number of different persons arrested or convicted and the total number committing offenses is, however, another matter. If there is a low probability of arrest for any one offense but the offender commits a large number of crimes in a short time, then the probability of arresting and convicting the offender may be high and the recidivism rates would become increasingly accurate as indicators of those who continue to commit crimes.

Corrections agencies also may try to enhance community adjustment or social functioning, yet except for employment (Measure 11) there appear to be no reliable techniques for measuring social functioning. Ethical and "logistical" problems in locating and interviewing discharged offenders make the assessment of long-term social adjustment in the community difficult and generally infeasible. (Some state officials may feel that follow-up attempts to interview persons discharged from parole or unconditionally discharged are unwarranted intrusions on privacy. Having paid their debts, offenders should not be subjected to what they may view as harassment or to possible revelation to employers or others that they are "ex-cons").

The following sections discuss how some periodic measurements of offender performance in the community might be made, with the foregoing limitations, on an annual basis and to identify some of the major problems in such measurement.

TO REDUCE CRIMINAL ACTIVITY

Although it is virtually impossible to measure the full extent of criminal activities of released offenders, no state corrections agency today regularly uses all of the reasonably accessible data to measure continued criminal activity, particularly data concerning offenders no longer on parole. Exhibit 10 summarizes practices of state corrections agencies in 1976 to measure recidivism. States frequently report and summarize the percentage of parolees who complete parole. Thirteen states annually report the percentage of offenders who return to the state's corrections agency within given periods of time after release from incarceration. No state systematically collects recidivism data and presents statistics specifically on offenders no longer under supervision to determine the long-term effects of corrections services. No state regularly obtains data on criminal activities (arrests or convictions) in other states to improve the reliability of recidivism statistics. Only two states use a recidivism measure based on new convictions within the state which do not necessarily lead to reincarceration in the state corrections facilities.

No one completely satisfactory measure for monitoring recidivism annually exists, nor was one developed in this project. Possible measures are suggested here, but each state corrections agency must adopt the option or options which—in light of data availability and the philosophy of the corrections agency—appear most appropriate. Measure 8 deals with criminal activity while on parole. Measure 9 deals with criminal activity *after* release from parole (or after unconditional discharge from prison without parole). Measure 10 focuses on recidivism rates for those reentering the

Exhibit 10
RECIDIVISM MEASURES USED BY STATE CORRECTIONS AGENCIES

Report of Findings from Interviews with 48[1] State Corrections Agencies

Measure	States Using Measure
Percentage of offenders entering correctional care with previous correctional record	26
Percentage of offenders leaving incarceration who return to prison in the same state within:	
1 year	7
15–18 months	1
2 years	6
3 years	14
5 years	3
Subtotal of states[2]	25
Number of these states reporting this type of recidivism annually	13
Special studies of percentage of offenders leaving incarceration who are subsequently rearrested; as reported by FBI RAP sheet	2
States with none of above three measures	5

1. Includes 47 states and the District of Columbia; excludes Alaska, Hawaii, and New Hampshire.

2. Some states use more than one time period.

SOURCE: Site visits to North Carolina and Wisconsin in 1975 and telephone survey of corrections offices of planning and evaluation by Louis Blair in April 1976.

state's prison system. There are many concerns in measuring recidivism, such as how much effort it takes to obtain data, what the indicators are of recidivism, and how many released inmates must be tracked. These specific issues are addressed in the supplement to this chapter.

The recidivism options suggested here differ somewhat from the recidivism measurement by the National Advisory Commission of Criminal Justice Standards and Goals.[1] It defined recidivism, in part, as "measured by (1) criminal acts that resulted in conviction by a court, when committed by individuals who are under correctional supervision or who have been released from correctional supervision within the previous three years. . . ." For the *annual monitoring*

_____

1. NACCJSG, *Corrections*, p. 513.

purpose, the recidivism options suggested in this study appear more practical than this NACCJSG recidivism measurement, primarily because they provide data in a much more timely way. They require a one-year rather than a three-year follow-up and they suggest the use of arrest data, which can be obtained sooner than conviction data.

Some types of offenders (for example, youthful auto thieves or burglars) are more likely to recidivate than others (such as embezzlers or murderers). Annual changes in recidivism rates due to corrections efforts might be masked by changes in the mix of offenders being released. Increases in rates might be due to a different mix of offenders being released and not to deterioration of the corrections program. Thus, corrections agencies monitoring "rehabilitation" should categorize recidivism statistics by "client difficulty," the likelihood that ex-offenders will recidivate. Such a categorization helps in comparing performance over time. This will be discussed later.

Measure 8: *Criminal involvement while under parole supervision, as measured by*

(*a*) *percentage of all offenders on parole in the past twelve months who are* arrested (*or whose arrests pass a preliminary hearing*) *for a criminal offense allegedly committed prior to completion of parole; or*
(*b*) *percentage of all offenders on parole in the past twelve months who are* convicted *of a criminal offense committed while on parole; or*
(*c*) *percentage of offenders who successfully complete parole without revocation for a criminal offense.*[2]

In most states, the majority of inmates released from incarceration are placed on parole. During parole they continue to receive supervision and, often, some type of supportive services or counseling to help them avoid criminal activities and to solve other problems.[3] Presumably these supportive parole services and the immediate threat of revocation affect the criminal behavior of released offenders and recidivism rates

probably will differ from the "after-care" or long-term recidivism rates of offenders no longer on parole or unconditionally released. The immediate or short-term success of correction services during the parole period can be measured with varying degrees of accuracy by the three options suggested. Measure 8a focuses on arrest data; Measure 8b, on conviction data; and Measure 8c, on parole revocation data. Each option has advantages and disadvantages, some of which are highlighted in exhibit 11.

Revocation of parole is used rather frequently as an indicator, but there are problems. On the one hand, parole can be revoked for technical reasons (violation of reporting requirements, failure to hold a job, unauthorized travel, and so forth) and such revocation would not necessarily indicate criminal behavior; a possible solution to this problem is to report only the revocations for criminal activity. On the other hand, some arrests and even convictions might not lead to parole revocation—possibly because (1) the offense is not considered serious enough to cause it, (2) the parole revocation authority does not learn of the activity, (3) the delays associated with revocation hearings are so long that parole expires, or (4) the offense is so serious that a trial is conducted (even if the parolee is convicted, there might not be a revocation). There are likely to be variations over time and among parole officials on what constitutes an offense serious enough to cause institution of revocation proceedings; considerations include lenient or strict attitudes on the part of individual parole officers or extenuating circumstances such as lack of room in prisons.[4]

A particularly attractive option for Measures 8 and 9 is to use high-quality arrest data—those arrests which have passed a preliminary hearing or which have resulted in arraignment. They are more likely to result in conviction (and to be acceptable as an indicator of guilt) than "unprocessed" arrest data. They are available without experiencing the long delays in waiting for courts to convict or to reincarcerate offenders.

If the options based on arrests or convictions are used, data probably would be gathered only for a random sample of parolees, because these options require special data-collection efforts. It has not been possible within the limited resources of this project to compare the three options as to what results each would yield and then to examine differences that appeared, but the comparison is highly desirable. For example, to determine how accurate the number of revo-

---

2. The actual form of "c" may vary, depending on the way parole and revocation data are reported. It could be either the percentage of all persons scheduled for release from parole in the past year who were released without ever being revoked: the percentage of all persons on parole in the past twelve months who were not terminated for parole revocation.

3. The most recent data available at the time the report was written showed that 77 percent of the inmates discharged from state corrections facilities in 1973 were released on parole. U.S. Department of Justice, Law Enforcement Assistance Administration, *Sourcebook of Criminal Justice Statistics, 1974*, p. 475.

---

4. For a discussion on variations in parole officer attitudes toward revocation, see Ohlin, Power, and Papperfort, "Major Dilemma of the Social Worker in Probation and Parole," *National Probation and Parole Association Journal*, 2(3):211–225, July 1956.

	Advantages	Disadvantages
Arrests	*Most rapid indication of criminal activity.* Corrections officials do not have to wait for court action which can take months to occur after arrest. At one time in the District of Columbia, the mean length of time from presentation to nontrial disposition[1] was 22 weeks, and it was 27 weeks for trial disposition. Similar, if not longer, delays are expected, at least in large urban areas. *Data on out-of-state arrests can be obtained through the FBI Identification Division Record System using RAP sheet data* (see exhibit 14). The RAP sheets often do not show case disposition, so conviction or reincarceration data would have to be obtained through personal follow-up. However, the delays that Missouri and North Carolina have experienced in getting RAP sheets suggest this procedure might be cumbersome for an annual monitoring effort. *Arrest records probably indicate more of the extent of criminal activity than do convictions or reincarcerations* (including parole revocation). Even though there is often not enough evidence to obtain a conviction or even to pass a preliminary hearing leading to a formal arrest, some persons feel that arrests still are more indicative of continued criminal activity than convictions.[2] Ethically and legally, it would be improper to declare (and punish) an individual offender as a recidivist based on arrests; but for estimating recidivism, there is no such problem. *"High quality" arrests—those that have passed a preliminary hearing and resulted in a formal charge being placed—generally lead to some type of conviction and could be used as quick, available proxy data avoiding some of the unreliability of raw arrest data. "High quality" arrest data are likely to be more difficult to obtain than raw arrest data.*	Data probably will have to be processed at least in part by hand because corrections files are unlikely to be linked with arrest files. Corrections agency probably will have to rely on another agency, such as the FBI or a state criminal justice agency, to provide arrest data. The quality of the data and the responsiveness in providing the data may be beyond the control of the corrections agency. Arrest does not indicate legal guilt. The offender may actually be innocent. Some governments may consider it unethical and improper to pass judgment on a group of offenders using only raw arrests. The use of "high quality" arrests might be acceptable.
Convictions	*With the highest certainty, indicates possible continued criminal activity.* Ethically, it seems likely to be acceptable to more officials than any other indicator.	Less sensitive than arrests. The long periods typically encountered between arrest and conviction or other court disposition means that longer follow-up periods have to be used than for arrests to obtain the same amount of "sensitivity." Then, it is also less responsive to the need for rapid feedback for annual monitoring efforts.

	Advantages	Disadvantages
(Convictions, cont'd)		Information on convictions in local courts and out-of-state courts will probably be very difficult to obtain. The FBI RAP sheet reporting system probably would have to be used and then follow-ups on arrests, conducted to identify convictions.
		Some of those who are guilty and arrested will not be convicted.
Revocations/ Reincarcerations	*Readily available for instate conviction or parole revocation.*	Less sensitive than arrests.
	Familiar to most corrections agencies.	Difficult to get information for federal, out-of-state, or local court convictions.
		Tends to indicate only the most severe offenses. Many felony convictions, particularly for property offenses, might not result in incarceration. Its accuracy in indicating continued criminal activity appears lower than arrests or convictions.
		FBI RAP sheets and state criminal justice information networks are believed to indicate incarceration only rarely, making follow-ups to obtain local court and out-of-state court data difficult.

1. *A Report to the President's Commission on Law Enforcement and the Administration of Justice,* Task Force Report, Science and Technology, Government Printing Office, 1967, p. 206.

2. There is no practical way to prove this statement; but it seems to be a strongly held contention among some persons in the criminal justice area. A number of corrections program evaluations have been based on arrest rates (Blumstein and Cohen, and Lenihan are recent ones; Lipton, et al., have noted some older studies that use arrests as indicators of recidivism).

cations is as an indicator of criminal involvement, it would be useful to examine a sample of parolees' records of convictions for offenses occurring during parole.

Measure 9: *Criminal involvement when no longer under correctional supervision, as measured by*

(a) *percentage of offenders* arrested *for (or whose arrests pass a preliminary hearing) a criminal offense within twelve months from completion of parole or unconditional discharge from incarceration;*

(b) *percentage of offenders* convicted *for a criminal offense within twelve months from parole revocation or unconditional discharge; or*

(c) *percentage of offenders reincarcerated for a criminal offense within twelve months from completion of parole or unconditional discharge from incarceration.*

If a state corrections agency accepts the objective of rehabilitation, then it seems appropriate to measure the extent of criminal activity *after* offenders leave all forms of correctional supervision, *including* parole, and to distinguish it from criminal activity while under parole.

As indicated earlier, no state systematically presents recidivism statistics specifically on offenders after they have finished their parole. Although twelve states present recidivism statistics for persons who have been released for from one to five years, they make no distinction between those on parole and those no longer on parole. State corrections agencies need to monitor this postservice performance aspect to obtain information on the longer term impacts of correctional programs.[5]

5. This suggestion is consistent with the definition of recidivism in NACCJSG, *Corrections,* p. 513, which considers recidivism as measured in part by criminal acts of individuals *who have been released from correctional supervision* (including release from parole) within the last three years.

As with Measure 8, three similar options are presented here. Measure 9a focuses on arrests or high quality arrests; Measure 9b, on convictions; and Measure 9c, on reincarcerations.

Measure 10. *Reincarceration: Number and percentage of offenders entering prison who have previously been incarcerated in the state prison system*

At least twenty-six state corrections agencies already summarize and report annually some reincarceration statistics. The main question is, what does this measure really indicate about corrections effectiveness? It seems to indicate the extent to which correctional authorities have been unable to prevent resumption of criminal activities by some offenders. Perhaps it is most useful as an indication of the client-difficulty issue; repeaters generally are difficult to rehabilitate. However, it does not indicate directly what percentage of previously released offenders are repeaters, as Measure 9 does (though with much more difficulty in data collection). Increases in the percentage of persons entering with previous convictions might occur because of decreases in the number of persons with no previous correctional experience who are being convicted and incarcerated. The *number* (rather than the percentage) of offenders reentering prison, thus is likely to be the more meaningful indicator, because that number will indicate the magnitude of the recidivism (in terms of incarcerations) problem in the state.

Other forms of this measure in use among states and indicating the inability of previous correctional experience to rehabilitate offenders include the number and percentage of incoming offenders with

- Incarceration within any state's correctional system, the Federal Bureau of Prisons, or military prisons
- Incarcerations only for prior felony convictions
- All correctional experience, whether it involved incarceration or probation in an adult or a juvenile system.

The percentage of persons *in the prison* with previous convictions should *not* be used as a measure of performance. As Reasons and Kaplan point out, "Repeat offenders receive longer sentences and are less likely to be paroled. Thus, they accumulate in prison and are disproportionately represented in any inmate population."[6]

Data for the suggested form can be obtained readily from corrections files in those states where offender records are filed centrally and retained for long periods. Some states—either for court action or for prison purposes—request FBI RAP sheets, which provide another check on the accuracy of state records as well as a source of information for incarcerations in other states. A few corrections agencies use only self-reports by the offender—data of questionable reliability. Because data on previous juvenile corrections experience are likely to be available only from the inmate, the reliability of the measure relating to all corrections experience is limited.

TO IMPROVE SOCIAL PRODUCTIVITY

Measure 11. *Percentage of offenders employed or otherwise socially productive (in school or job training, meeting family responsibilities) full time when released from parole*

Many corrections agencies devote substantial efforts toward enhancing the capability of mentally and physically able offenders to be employed or otherwise socially productive full time in the community. The goal is twofold: to reduce offenders' need to commit crimes to raise money, and to assist them in becoming integrated into the community. Corrections' influence on employment seems likely to be relatively low compared to the influence of the local and national economy and other exogenous factors. Still, this measure is important, for it tries to establish whether rehabilitative opportunities offered to offenders in prison or on parole exert lasting influence.

There is a question as to when to assess social productivity. Preferably, the assessment would be done some time after release from parole—perhaps twelve months after—to determine if rehabilitative efforts have had lasting effects. Probably the best way to get such data would be through follow-up interviews with a randomly selected sample of former offenders. The difficulty and frequent infeasibility of conducting follow-ups are discussed in Chapter I. However, in one study, a success rate of 70 percent was achieved in locating and interviewing offenders; the cost was about $170 per interview and took a year of calendar time.[7] These costs seem higher than what most corrections agencies can spend with the limited time and resources they have for monitoring. One probable bias

---

6. C. E. Reasons and R. L. Kaplan, "Tear Down the Walls? Some Functions of Prisons," *Crime and Delinquency,* October 1975, pp. 368–372

7. Ann D. Witte, "Work Release in North Carolina." Witte summarizes some of the findings from work-release programs which attempt to upgrade social productivity; she also presents findings of her own suggesting that improved productivity has, in some cases, reduced either the severity of criminal activity or the extent of recidivism.

to the data-collection procedure is that, except for offenders who have been reincarcerated, the offenders with good social adjustment and employment patterns are the easiest to locate. If, in fact, the persons interviewed are not similar in employment to those in the sample who could not be interviewed, the indicated success rate will be too high and the measure of relatively low reliability. One way to avoid this problem and to provide conservative values is to count all those who could not be located for interviews as unemployed in determining the percentage.

A measure of employment at the time of release from parole generally will be more practical. Parole officers often document parolee employment and income information in the case files (although the accuracy and timeliness of this information depends on such factors as the parole officer's workload and parolee reporting requirements). In spite of the presence of data concerning social productivity in case files, Wisconsin apparently is the only state to produce summary statistics periodically on employment of all persons leaving parole.[8] Some other states make a final assessment of offenders before they are discharged from parole, but they do not summarize the findings. Wisconsin has published statistics on the percentage of all persons who, at the time their parole ended, were employed (full time or part time) plus the average income per month.[9] California, Texas, Minnesota, and Florida conduct periodic program evaluations of social productivity for offenders who have been in vocational education programs, but these make up only a small proportion of the total number released on parole.

Data could be collected from assessments by parole officers if such information is reliable. If the data are not sufficiently reliable, much more tedious special investigations—perhaps taking one-half to one day of staff time per case—would be needed for a minimum of 100 to 200 cases.[10]

_____

8. In 1976, Michigan and Illinois were developing data-processing and computer-based information systems that could provide such summary data on employment of all persons at the time of release from parole.

9. See, for example, "1972 Probation and Parole Termination," Statistical Bulletin C-56, Wisconsin Department of Corrections.

10. To check the reliability of agency records on employment and social productivity before using them for monitoring, special investigators could select 100 to 200 parolee cases at random, and determine the parolees' social productivity, possibly by interviewing the offenders or their families and by contacting the employers. These findings then could be compared with the case files of parole officers for compatibility. The parole officers' records might be considered sufficiently accurate for this measure if for at least 90 percent of the cases they agree with the special investigation findings on employment.

This suggested measure provides only a limited assessment of employment and productivity—a one-time, snapshot view at the end of parole. Ex-offenders appear to have greater employment problems than other citizens and to shift more frequently among jobs, so they may have frequent periods of unemployment. Hence a snapshot view of one offender's social productivity might be misleading; although for a large group, there should be no major problem. The suggested measure appears to be a reasonable compromise among ease of data collection, reliability of the information, and meaningfulness of the data. It does not, however, reveal longer term adjustment.

Some states have an indeterminate parole period during which, except in very unusual circumstances, parole is not terminated unless the parolee is socially productive. In states where this undefined term is the general rule, the suggested measure would not be appropriate. Follow-ups or some of the measures described below would have to be employed to monitor social productivity.

Other Measures of Social Productivity

Though they appear less appropriate for annual monitoring than the suggested measure, some other possibilities for measures follow:

- *Percentage of time offenders were socially productive in the six months (or twelve months) prior to release from parole.* This figure avoids the snapshot-view problem of the suggested measure, but it would be more difficult to obtain and to verify, particularly in the cases of offenders whom parole officers cannot monitor closely because of case overloads or because of the nature of the parole-reporting requirements. Moreover, for persons on short-term parole (six to twelve months perhaps), employment patterns in the first few months after release from prison might not be stable and therefore would be unrepresentative of their longer term employment patterns.

- *Income: Average weekly or annual earned income at release from parole.* This measure, though frequently used in ad hoc studies and program evaluations, appears less appropriate than the other measures described. It covers only persons who have income-producing jobs; it is probably more susceptible to change with different mixes of clients; it needs adjustments for inflation in annual comparisons; and it probably is more difficult to collect accurately.

- *Percentage of offenders who are self-supporting at release from parole.* Self-supporting might be defined as meeting all income needs from earned income, and not from supplemental sources such as food stamps, public assistance, rent support, or family assistance. There could be a problem in considering a person as self-supporting if he/she meets all his/her financial needs but lives in substandard housing or has inadequate food or medical attention. It has the advantage over Measure 11 in that marginal employment counted under Measure 11 would not be counted here. It avoids some of the difficulties of collecting accurate income data, but it excludes those who do not have income-producing jobs but still are engaged in socially productive activities. Also, it might not be appropriate to apply to persons who could meet their own needs if they did not have financial responsibilities to other family members.

- *Percentage of offenders working in jobs (or otherwise socially productive) at or close to their vocational potential.* Ericson has been credited with an approach to measuring vocational productivity which could be appropriate in a sampling-monitoring procedure.[11] For this measure, vocational experts would rate a sample of offenders on the basis of vocational achievement, or current job, compared to individual potential. This measure would probably be the most expensive form and seems more appropriate for evaluation of special programs than for monitoring.
- *Miscellaneous measures.* Other possible measures are progress in job (raises or more responsibility), or length of time on one job. These would seem to be less appropriate or important for annual monitoring than the other measures suggested.

Before-and-After Comparisons

Measure 11 indicates the "current" status of offenders. The corrections agency might want to establish before-and-after comparative measures to indicate changes in status. Examples would be differences in the percentage of offenders socially productive full time at arrest and at their release from parole, and the average change in the annual income (in constant dollars) of individual inmates from the year prior to arrest to the year prior to release from parole. The income would have to be extrapolated to an annual rate for those offenders incarcerated for some portion of the year prior to their arrest or not on parole for a full year prior to release. Because it may be difficult to obtain reliable data (other than offender self-reports) on conditions before coming into corrections custody (such as income and percentage of the year employed), it may not be practical to use before-and-after measures of change for annual monitoring. The data on social productivity during parole often can be verified through examining paychecks, investigating the family, and possibly contacting the employer.

What Client-Difficulty Groups Should Be Established

In addition to the stigma of a criminal conviction which can diminish employability, some parolees will have more undesirable employment characteristics than others. These include few marketable skills, low education levels, poor work habits (perhaps exacerbated by long periods of inactivity while incarcerated), and residence in communities with high unemployment rates.

To be able to track changes in social productivity and to judge whether they are due to changes in the types of offenders or in program or local economy effects, it is desirable to establish groupings for difficulty of parole employment. An illustrative threefold classification follows:

(1) *Most difficult.* No marketable skills, poor work habits and a long history of unemployment, high unemployment rates for unskilled persons in parolee's community.
(2) *Moderately difficult.* No marketable skills, or skills but poor work habits, or skills or willingness to work but high unemployment rates for persons with parolee's characteristics in parolee's community.
(3) *Least difficult.* Good employment history and willingness to work, opportunities for employment, education, meeting family requirements or otherwise being socially productive.

If it is considered too cumbersome to present the data for each difficulty group, the data could be presented for the entire set of persons leaving parole but with information added as to the percentage of the persons leaving parole in each client-difficulty group (or perhaps with the average rating based on a scale of 1, most difficult, to 3, least difficult).

---

11. See Lipton, Martinson, and Wilks, *The Effectiveness of Correctional Treatment,* pp. 338–339. This refers to Richard C. Ericson et al., "The Application of Comprehensive Psycho-Social Vocational Services in the "Rehabilitation of Parolees."

SUPPLEMENT TO CHAPTER III
Some Issues in Measuring Recidivism

The specific recidivism measures which the corrections agency uses for annual monitoring will depend primarily on how it resolves the seven concerns discussed below.

1. How Much Effort Is Required to Obtain the Data?

The amount of effort required to develop recidivism statistics for annual monitoring depends primarily on the particular measures selected, accessibility of data, and the number of records of released offenders that are tracked. If the data used are the type generally available within the corrections agency (parole revocation or reincarceration for a new conviction), and if the data collection can be automated, relatively little effort would be required to obtain overall recidivism statistics. If the data are grouped by client difficulty as suggested earlier, however, perhaps one to two hours would be required to classify each inmate using a procedure such as described in (5) below. If this client-difficulty assessment is not done in conjunction with regular prison and discharge processing, the additional effort could be so time consuming that only a sample of a few hundred might be classified to develop recidivism statistics. If arrest records are used—either from the FBI RAP sheets[12] (a sample RAP sheet is exhibit 15, and an explanation of its use appear below) or arrest records from a statewide criminal justice reporting system—the amount of time required to track *all* of the released offenders is likely to be great (and a large number—more than 200 to 300 in a batch—might overwhelm the rapid-response capability of the FBI). Data collection probably will be even more time consuming if arrests that have passed a preliminary hearing (high-quality arrests) or convictions are used as indicators of continued criminal activity. Thus, follow-up on only a sample of released offenders probably will have to be used in all but the smallest corrections system (perhaps those which release fewer than 300 inmates each year). As this relatively complex data-collection procedure has not been tested in this project, these estimates of the amount of effort required annually are crude.

2. Should Arrests, Convictions, or Revocation/Reincarcerations Be Used as Indicators of Continued Criminal Activity? (See Exhibit 11.)

The difficulty of detecting criminal activity complicates the accurate measuring of recidivism. Generally either subsequent arrests or convictions are used as evidence of such crime in special research or program evaluations, whereas corrections agencies reporting recidivism statistics usually employ reincarcerations. But most offenses do not lead to arrest, conviction, or reincarceration as illustrated by an FBI analysis on the disposition of known offenses.[13] An adult arrest was made for only 17.4 percent of the offenses; an adult conviction was obtained for the offense as charged in 4.8 percent of the offenses, and a conviction for a lesser offense in 0.9 percent of the offenses.[14] Five percent of the offenses resulted in a referral to a juvenile court. Statistics for felonies of homicide, robbery, and burglary in Los Angeles showed that in only 12.8 percent of the cases there was an arrest, in 4.0 percent there was a formal charge placed, in 2.5 percent there was a conviction, and for only 0.6 percent of the crimes reported was the offender sent to prison.[15]

Thus, figures on arrests, convictions, and incarcerations provide only a partial count of the criminal acts being committed by previously convicted offenders. It is important, however, to keep in mind that a major function of the measurements is to indicate changes over time. Hence, even though a substantial

---

12. For a more extensive discussion of this system, see the *Federal Register*, (40) 167:38771-2.

13. U.S. Department of Justice, *Crime in the United States, Uniform Crime Reports*, 1971, p. 11.

14. Many crimes are not reported. The Law Enforcement Assistance Administration report, *Criminal Justice Surveys in 13 American Cities*, p. 114, showed that, for example, in Milwaukee, the percentages of crimes reported to the police were: 34 percent of all crimes in the personal sector (rape, robbery, assault); 45 percent in the household sector (burglary and larceny); and 84 percent in the commercial sector (burglary and robbery).

15. Los Angeles Police Department, Criminal Justice System Monitoring Unit, *California Criminal Justice System Analysis*. Statistics from the U.S. Department of Justice, *Crime in the United States, 1974*, p. 47, showed that 21 percent of the Index crimes committed in 1974 were cleared: 81 percent of the adults arrested for indexed crimes were prosecuted, and of the 81 percent, 61 percent were found guilty as charged and 9 percent were found guilty of a lesser charge. Assuming that all clearances resulted in arrests, only 12 percent of the *reported* offenses led to conviction. (And the percentage incarcerated for such offenses would be substantially lower.)

amount of recidivism is not detected by these measures; the data still can indicate major trends.

The accuracy of recidivism tallies seems likely to vary according to the nature of the offense and the offenders. They are perhaps least inaccurate for indicating the portion who continue in extensive criminal activity, those who commit many crimes and thus presumably have a much higher probability of being apprehended than if they had committed only one offense, those who are least skilled at avoiding arrest, and those who commit crimes such as murder that have relatively high probabilities of being reported and cleared by arrest.

Whether arrests, convictions, or reincarcerations are used, it is desirable to obtain information on out-of-state criminal involvement to estimate more accurately the extent of recidivism. According to FBI statistics, more than half of the 207,748 offenders arrested nationwide for a federal offense in 1974 had been arrested in more than one state.[16] This rate suggests a high degree of mobility, at least among felons. Recidivism statistics based only on in-state arrests, convictions, or reincarcerations will probably substantially underestimate continued, known criminal activity. A possible approach is to obtain FBI RAP sheets on a sample of released offenders to determine what percentage of criminal actions are being detected in state and what percentage are out of state.

To reduce the likelihood that data on arrests includes arrests only by very weak evidence, it would be preferable to consider only those arrests that had survived the first judicial screening.[17] Currently, however, state information systems do not generally collect this information.

3. How Long a Period Without Another Criminal Incident Is Necessary to Define the Offender as a Nonrecidivist for the Purpose of This Measure?

The length of time used for follow-ups has varied from as little as six months to as much as five years. The NACCJSG *Corrections* volume recommends three years—a period which seems unduly long for annual monitoring. (An agency probably would have

to wait at least four years to obtain recidivism data.) The Division of Planning and Research in the South Carolina Department of Corrections, which uses a three-year follow-up period, was not able to publish recidivism statistics on 1972 releases until March 22, 1976.

Recidivism rates will be higher as longer periods of time are included. To provide some timely feedback to public officials, however, some reasonably early cut-off time is needed. Aspects to consider in selecting a period include:

- How long should the corrections agency be held accountable for recidivism? Should it be expected to keep an offender from return to crime for, say, three years after release from parole?
- How long does it take for most recidivism to be detected?

The first aspect can be determined only by the state. With regard to the second aspect, there seems to be wide variation; a special analysis of recidivism, based only on rearrests and published in the *Uniform Crime Reports, 1970,* showed that 62.5 percent of a group of 16,332 offenders released to the community were rearrested by the end of the fourth calendar year after release.[18] But 42.7 percent (or *68 percent of the recidivists*) were rearrested within one year of release and 52.5 percent (or *84 percent of the recidivists*) were rearrested within two years. These figures should be viewed with caution, however, because they were based only on rearrests.

Exhibit 12 shows recidivism rates (based on reincarcerations for both new convictions and parole revocations) for the states of Washington and South Carolina. The Washington recidivism data (exhibit 12A) suggest that approximately half of those who develop into recidivists return within an average of one year. On the other hand, the South Carolina data (exhibit 12B) show that after the first six months, the return rate is fairly constant and that substantially less than half (36.3 percent) of the recidivism occurs in the first year.[19] If the South Carolina experience is the more typical, a longer follow-up time period would seem preferable. These data refer only to reconvictions; because arrests would have shown up sooner, the figures would be considerably higher for arrests.

Blumstein and Cohen present rearrest statistics for individuals who were arrested (but not incarcer-

---

16. U.S. Department of Justice, *Crime in the United States 1974*, p. 48. Yet a recent study by Ann D. Witte indicates that only 10 percent of reincarcerations of a selected sample of released offenders occurred outside the states in which the offenders were originally incarcerated.

17. The advantages and procedures for obtaining such data are discussed in *Opportunities for Improving Productivity in Police Services*, The National Commission on Productivity, 1973, and "How Effective Are Your Community Services?", The Urban Institute, Hatry, *et al.*, forthcoming 1977.

18. U.S. Department of Justice, *Crime in the United States, 1970*, p. 40.

19. The reasons for the difference in recidivism rates are not known. It could be that the length of time to obtain a conviction in South Carolina is substantially longer rather than that in Washington or that there are substantial differences in criminal behavior of released offenders in the two states.

Exhibit 12A
PERSONS PAROLED OR DISCHARGED FROM WASHINGTON STATE ADULT CORRECTIONS, 1965–1974, WHO HAVE RETURNED TO STATE INCARCERATION

| Year of Release | Number Released | Percentage Returning Within: | | | | | | Percentage Returned As of June 1975* |
		6 mo.	1 yr.	2 yrs.	3 yrs.	4 yrs.	5 yrs.	
1965	1,273	10.1	21.3	30.3	35.0	37.8	39.3	42.7
1966	1,357	6.9	15.8	27.7	33.5	36.3	37.4	40.0
1967	1,673	7.3	16.5	27.7	31.4	32.9	34.1	36.5
1968	1,490	7.2	18.7	29.7	33.9	35.9	36.8	39.1
1969	1,503	8.8	18.4	29.2	33.7	36.1	37.3	38.2
1970	1,380	6.4	15.1	24.5	28.8	31.1	*	32.8
1971	1,593	5.0	13.2	23.0	27.9	*	*	30.8
1972	1,736	5.0	13.7	22.8	*	*	*	27.7
1973	1,490	6.0	12.7	*	*	*	*	21.9
1974	1,363	6.1	*	*	*	*	*	12.8
TOTAL	14,858	6.8	*	*	*	*	*	32.2

* All populations were followed through June 30, 1975. The entire 1965 population was followed for 9½ years while those released at the end of 1974 could only be followed for six months. The June 30, 1975 follow-up allows for an "average" follow-up of one year for the 1974 population (some persons had been "at risk" 18 months while others had been released for only six months).

SOURCE: Ralph W. Smith, *Who Returns? A Study of Recidivism for Adult Offenders in the State of Washington*, Olympia, Wash.: Department of Social and Health Services Planning and Research Division, 1976, p. 6.

Exhibit 12B
TIME BETWEEN RELEASE AND READMISSION OF SOUTH CAROLINA DEPARTMENT OF CORRECTIONS 1972 RELEASEES RECIDIVATED WITHIN THREE YEARS

Time Gap Between Release and Readmission	Number of Recidivists	Percentage of Recidivists
0–6 months	88	22.3
7–12 months	55	14.0
13–18 months	57	14.5
19–24 months	64	16.2
25–30 months	67	17.0
31–36 months	63	16.0

SOURCE: *Study to Determine the Recidivism Rate for the South Carolina Department of Corrections' Calendar Year 1972 Releases*, p. 3.

ated) twice in two years.[20] Their data show that nearly 80 percent of the rearrests took place within twelve months of unconditional release or end of parole and 55 percent within six months.

A more definite answer for a particular state on how long it takes for the bulk of recidivism to show up could be obtained by comparing the rearrest dates, the reconviction or reincarceration dates, and the initial dates of release to the community of a sample of several hundred recidivists to estimate the percentage who might be expected to be picked up in various follow-up periods—perhaps six, twelve, or twenty-four months. However, this relationship cannot necessarily be expected to remain stable in the future. If it is used to set the follow-up period, it should be rechecked periodically.

Because of the anticipated difficulty in collecting data based on arrest or convictions, it would appear feasible to use only one follow-up period, preferably twelve months. This period would appear sufficient to detect much criminal activity, and would avoid unduly long delays in providing overall performance data.

4. How Should the Severity of the New Offense Be Handled?

The NACCJSG *Corrections* definition recommends that the recidivism measure indicate the sever-

---

20. Blumstein and Cohen, *An Evaluation of a College-level Program*, p. 162.

ity of the new offenses. It is desirable to know if the criminal behavior is more or less severe after correctional services. But most criminal activity does not result in arrests, convictions, or reincarcerations, and because convictions are sometimes the result of plea bargaining, the final charge does not necessarily indicate the full severity of the offense committed. The available indicators of continued criminal activity do not appear sufficiently accurate to provide data for annual monitoring. *Hence it is not suggested that monitoring procedures attempt to indicate the seriousness of new offenses.* Such fine tuning of inherently inaccurate data implies a precision in recidivism statistics that does not really exist. Still, some state corrections agencies might want to monitor outcomes other than arrested/not arrested, convicted/not convicted, or reincarcerated/not reincarcerated. There are several scales that can be used to indicate outcome seriousness.[21]

5. *How Does an Agency Account for Offenders with Different Rehabilitation Probabilities? (The "Client Difficulty" Issue)*

Some classes of offenders have been found to be more likely to be apprehended for new criminal offenses than others. Thus, the recidivism tallies preferably should indicate outcomes for "more difficult to rehabilitate" cases as distinguished from "less difficult to rehabilitate" cases. This type of breakdown is particularly useful when the mix of inmates released (either unconditionally or on parole) may change substantially from year to year. Without accounting for the types of offenders, it would be difficult to know if changes are due to differences in offenders (that is, more or less "difficult" cases being released) rather than to other factors such as changes in the quality of correctional services.

Statistical analyses of recidivists by Daniel Glaser and Vincent O'Leary, by Don Gottfredson, and by others indicate five characteristics that are correlated relatively highly with recidivism:[22]

- Type of offense
- Prior record
- Duration of prior criminality
- Severe drug or alcohol involvement
- Age at intake to and at release from correctional custody.

The characteristics of the offenders at release might be used to classify them into perhaps four levels of client difficulty or likelihood of recidivism. A relatively simple approach would be to use "expert judgment" (such as the judgments of parole board officials and perhaps some corrections experts not employed by the state corrections agency) to establish specific ground rules for assigning each released offender into one of, say, four categories of case difficulty (based on that person's characteristics as discussed above).[23]

A more quantitative and probably more reliable approach—though still with limitations—is to estimate from a multiple regression analysis of recidivism rates of a large number of offenders (perhaps 1,000 or more) the influence each factor has on the likelihood for recidivism.[24] This task is likely to be very difficult, requiring more personnel and data-processing resources than most corrections agencies can devote to it. Alternatively, one could use the results of a "Base Expectancy Score" (BES) analysis such as that in use by the California Department of Corrections, which was developed by such a statistical analysis.

The BES approach is illustrated by Kassebaum, Ward, and Wilner, who grouped offenders into four categories.[25] The scoring was based on conditions of the offenders at intake for their current commitment—as detected through files—and the weightings developed by a regression analysis. The four groupings, the conditions, and their relative weighting are shown in exhibit 13. (Note that the BES scale does not use age, education, or race, factors shown to be correlated at times with recidivism.) The higher the score, the better the prognosis for completing parole successfully.

A client-difficulty grouping could be developed using data from these factors, using similar data from other base-expectancy and parole-survival studies, or using data developed in conjunction with an in-depth recidivism study in a particular state. Gene Kasse-

---

21. See, for example, David Moberg and Richard Ericson, "A New Recidivism Outcome Index," *Federal Probation,* June 1972, pp. 50–57; T. Sellin and M. E. Wolfgang, *The Measurement of Delinquency;* and Peter Hoffman *et al.,* "The Practical Application of a Severity Scale," pp. 28–29. The North Carolina Department of Correction utilizes sentence length as a measure of severity, primarily for planning purposes.

22. Characteristics associated with recidivism are discussed in U.S. Department of Justice, *Crime in the United States, 1974,* pp. 45–54; Daniel Glaser and Vincent O'Leary, "Personal Characteristics and Parole Outcomes," and Don Gottfredson *et al.,* "4000 Lifetimes."

23. Another classification procedure which might be useful to state corrections agencies has been developed by L. T. Wilkins and J. MacNaughton-Smith, "New Prediction and Classification Methods in Criminology," in *Probation and Parole Selected Readings.*

24. In a separate project, the North Carolina Department of Correction developed a model of recidivism based on such a multivariate analysis.

25. Gene Kassebaum, David Ward, and David Wilner, *Prison Treatment and Parole Survival,* p. 254.

Exhibit 13

COMPONENTS AND RELATIVE WEIGHTING FOR BASE EXPECTANCY OF SUCCESSFUL PAROLE OUTCOME AND CLIENT-DIFFICULTY GROUPINGS

Based on Conditions at Intake

A. Components and Weights (to be applied to each offender)	Relative Weight
Arrest-free period of five or more years prior to current admission	12
No history of any opiate use	9
Few jail commitments (none, one, or two)	8
Present commitment is not on a charge of burglary or bad checks	7
No one in family has a criminal record	6
No alcohol involvement	6
First arrest was not for auto theft	5
Six months or more in any one job	5
No aliases	5
First commitment to prison	5
Favorable living arrangement prior to intake	4
Few prior arrests (none, one, or two)	4

B. Client-Difficulty Groupings

Very low BES	(0–23)	(Most likely to recidivate; i.e., most difficult to rehabilitate)
Medium low BES	(24–38)	
Medium high BES	(39–53)	
Very high BES	(over 53)	(Least likely to recidivate; i.e., least difficult to rehabilitate)

SOURCE: Kassebaum, *et al.*, *Prison Treatment*, p. 332.

baum and his associates showed that a base-expectancy type rating for four categories of client difficulty could predict about 40 percent to 50 percent of the variation. This rate is believed to be substantially better than could be arrived at by expert judgment, but it is also time-consuming.

Exhibit 14 illustrates the use of client-difficulty categories. Note that though the overall recidivism rates have decreased over time in the illustration, for all client-difficulty groups the rates have worsened. What happened is, that in 1975, many more of those tracked fell into the low-difficulty group. The last column on the right shows the average of base-expectancy scores to indicate the overall difficulty levels.

6. How Are Arrest or Conviction Data Obtained?

A major problem in measuring recidivism is how to obtain arrest or conviction data. The FBI Identification Division Records System is currently the primary feasible source for obtaining out-of-state criminal arrests and convictions data; and it may be the only source for comprehensive in-state arrest data, if there is no state criminal justice information system routinely recording all arrests. It issues the so-called RAP sheet shown in exhibit 15. The system files fingerprints, arrests, and convictions records of individuals who have been arrested or incarcerated by federal, state, or local law enforcement agencies. In theory, all persons fingerprinted for a criminal offense are included in the files and the information is available to state corrections agencies. Some agencies routinely request RAP sheets on all incoming offenders. The FBI will assist state agencies in recidivism studies by providing RAP sheets when the agency submits the name of each individual and his/her FBI number—data which generally should be available in corrections files. The FBI has assisted recidivism studies for the Missouri and Ohio corrections agencies. It tracked 10,000 persons for a special recidivism study by the U.S. Bureau of Prisons.

One member of the FBI Identification Division Records System informally reported that it would take up to three months to provide RAP sheets for a requested follow-up on 300 released offenders. There is no available information on the completeness of the files—in particular whether all or virtually all arrests and fingerprints are actually submitted to the FBI. Apparently some states might file these only with their own state criminal justice agencies for known recidivists and not transmit them to the FBI. The FBI received only about half as many RAP sheets as there were arrests made in 1974, but if most persons arrested are charged with more than one offense, then one RAP sheet could cover multiple offenses. The FBI employee did not know of any studies or data relating to the reliability of the RAP sheets. He did not believe that misclassification of fingerprints would be a problem affecting the accuracy of the reporting system. (The number of follow-ups needed is discussed in the next section.)

Exhibit 14
ILLUSTRATIVE DISPLAY OF RECIDIVISM[1] STATISTICS WITH CLIENT-DIFFICULTY RATING

Year of Release	BES Scores[2]								Total Released	Overall Recidivism %	Average BES Score
	Very High		Medium High		Medium Low		Very Low				
	No. Released	Recidivism (%)	No. Released	Recidivism (%)	No. Released	Recidivism (%)	No. Released	Recidivism (%)			
1975	230	22	170	26	125	35	75	54	600	30	48
1974	140	21	160	25	175	31	125	49	600	31	40
1973	60	15	110	22	200	30	230	45	600	33	34

1. Recidivism as used herein is reincarceration within twelve months of release from parole.
2. Relative client difficulty is determined by the offender's base expectancy score using the same categories as shown in exhibit 13, part B. A high BES score indicates a relatively favorable prognosis for rehabilitation and a relatively low likelihood of recidivating.

The director of a Missouri recidivism study using RAP sheets confirmed that it had taken him about three months, as well as several requests, to obtain RAP sheets for a random sample of 300 released offenders. The sheets were somewhat hard to interpret and information on arrest disposition (conviction, dismissal, reduction in charge) frequently was missing. Arrests appeared to be up to date. It took approximately one person-month to review the RAP sheets and to extract the recidivism figures—both in terms of arrests and of convictions. Because the state did not have an extensive automated data system, it had taken more staff time to draw the sample and to obtain FBI numbers from the state corrections file than it did to extract the data from the RAP sheets. North Carolina Department of Correction officials also reported difficulties in obtaining RAP sheets for incoming offenders.

If arrests passing a preliminary hearing or convictions are used as the measure, then follow-up calls are likely to be required. The RAP sheets do not always indicate disposition or quality of arrest. The state's criminal justice information system might have data on convictions which did not necessarily lead to reincarceration. There was too little time and staff available during this project to examine the quality of and accessibility to data in state criminal justice information networks, but such an examination should take place before a decision is made to rely on such information for measuring recidivism. This study probably will involve manual analysis of the data. The corrections agency itself, particularly if it has a centralized prison and probation file, will be a readily available source of conviction data and possibly could be programmed for automatic computation of recidivism statistics. The completeness of the corrections agency file and of any state's information file could be estimated by drawing a random sample of former inmates, requesting RAP sheets, arrest, and conviction records from any state criminal justice information system, and corrections agency files on the sample, and comparing the findings with one another.

7. How Many Released Inmates Should Be Tracked?

If statistics are developed for arrests or for convictions (but not for reincarcerations), a sampling approach is suggested. A random sample of offenders released during the period of concern would be selected.[26] Their arrest or conviction records would be examined to determine known criminal activity. For annual monitoring purposes, sampling can reduce substantially the amount of effort required with little practical sacrifice in accuracy. This process is different from that used by most state corrections agencies, which attempt to track *all* offenders released in a particular year to develop overall recidivism statistics. Research personnel in several states without automated data-reporting systems (South Carolina, Massachusetts, Florida, and Rhode Island) reported this task to be difficult and time-consuming.

How many cases need to be checked to obtain results with reasonable accuracy? A sample size of 100

26. A statistically sound method of sample selection should be developed. North Carolina obtained an alphabetical listing of all offenders in the population group of interest and then selected every tenth person on the list. The sample selected should be checked for representativeness—perhaps by comparing its race, age, and type of offense statistics with those of the general population to see if they are similar. If there are substantial dissimilarities, another sample should be drawn and checked. This task should be relatively simple if the department has an automated data-processing capability.

Exhibit 15
SAMPLE FEDERAL BUREAU OF INVESTIGATION "RAP" SHEET

UNITED STATES DEPARTMENT OF JUSTICE
FEDERAL BUREAU OF INVESTIGATION
IDENTIFICATION DIVISION
WASHINGTON, D.C.   20537
FICTITIOUS RECORD

The following FBI record, NUMBER 000 000 X   , is furnished FOR OFFICIAL USE ONLY. Information shown on this Identification Record represents data furnished FBI by fingerprint contributors. WHERE DISPOSITION IS NOT SHOWN OR FURTHER EXPLANATION OF CHARGE OR DISPOSITION IS DESIRED, COMMUNICATE WITH AGENCY CONTRIBUTING THOSE FINGERPRINTS.

CONTRIBUTOR OF FINGERPRINTS	NAME AND NUMBER	ARRESTED OR RECEIVED	CHARGE	DISPOSITION
SO Clanton AL	John Doe A–000	3–9–65	susp	rel
SO Clanton AL	John J. Doe A–000	6–11–65	vag	rel
SO Clanton AL	John J. Joe A–000	9–18–65	intox	$25 or 25 das; pd
PD Montgomery AL	Joseph Doe CC–000	6–11–66	forg	
St Bd of Corr Montgomery AL	John Joseph Doe C–00000	10–18–66	forg 2nd deg	2 yrs & 1 day par 5–15–67
St Bd of Corr Montgomery AL	Joseph John Doe C–00000	returned 9–5–67	PV (forg 2nd deg)	to serve un–expired term of 2 yrs & 1 day
PD Montgomery AL	John Doe A–0000	2–20–68	burg & escapee	TOT St Bd of Corr Montgomery AL
St Bd of Corr Montgomery AL	John J. Doe C–00000	returned 2–21–68	burg & escapee	2 yrs
USM Jacksonville FL	John J. Doe 00–C	10–14–70	ITSMV	
USP Lewisburg PA	John Joseph Doe 00–NE	11–15–70	ITSMV	18 mos par 8–1–71

to 150 randomly selected cases for each category of offenders can provide statistics of sufficient accuracy for most monitoring purposes. This size group allows detecting differences of roughly 5 to 10 percentage points with a 90 percent confidence factor (that is, depending on the percentage of arrests of one of the samples, differences of 5 to 10 percentage points between two samples represent actual differences between the two populations and are not due to sampling chance). A simple null-hypothesis test can be conducted to determine if the differences are statistically significant. Some agencies might want to be able to identify smaller differences (3 to 5 percentage points) as being statistically significant. These agencies would need to use sample sizes of about 200 to 300.

If statistics are to be generated on (1) unconditional releases, (2) offenders who completed parole, and (3) offenders placed on parole, and if the measure is computed for each of four client-difficulty levels within each category, there would be twelve possible client groupings, or 1,200 to 1,800 persons to track. There will not be enough released offenders for all twelve groupings for smaller corrections agencies, and there may be data-collection difficulties for larger

agencies. If so, recidivism statistics might be generated only for each of the three release categories and not for each level of client difficulty within each category. However, this measure should still estimate the client difficulty of each sample—perhaps showing an average base-expectancy score as illustrated in exhibit 14.

For the twenty relatively small state corrections agencies discharging fewer than 1,000 adult inmates each year, it would be sufficient to examine randomly selected samples of perhaps 100 to 150 offenders placed on parole in the past twelve months, 100 to 150 released from parole in the past twelve months and, if there are substantial numbers of unconditional releases, 100 to 150 of those released in the past twelve months.[27] An average client-difficulty rating score would be computed. For the larger corrections agencies, perhaps the "full" 1,200 to 1,800 would be tracked annually to get recidivism data on each of four client-difficulty groupings.

---

27. For the number of inmates discharged by states, see U.S. Department of Justice, *Sourcebook of Criminal Justice Statistics, 1974*, pp. 475–477.

CHAPTER IV

IMPLEMENTATION ISSUES AND MEASUREMENT COSTS

STEPS IN IMPLEMENTING A MEASUREMENT SYSTEM

The set of measures described in this report has never been implemented in its entirety. Therefore the authors of this study cannot address from practical experience all of the major issues likely to be encountered, the steps that need to be followed to implement the entire set, and the total costs or staff time required to implement the procedures and to collect and analyze the data annually. Some of the experiences in developing and testing the measurement procedures are discussed in Appendix B. A substantial amount of time, perhaps a year of full-time work by one to three analysts, as well as the steps discussed below, are likely to be required in each state to implement the measurement capability.

1. Decide Which Measures Are Appropriate

Decisions on appropriate measures will involve personnel from the corrections agency, parole services (if separate from corrections), the state planning agency for criminal justice, the governor's office and from such "outside" users as the budget office, and possibly the legislative committees with corrections-oversight responsibilities. Discussion probably will cover the proper objectives for corrections services and the appropriateness of monitoring rehabilitation; resources available for measurement and for correcting any problems likely to be uncovered; current performance reporting; perceived problem areas; and needs for data. The measures contained in this report might be used as a starting point. It is important to give many persons in the state's correction agency the opportunity to participate in the decisions, because they are more likely to use a set of measures developed with their cooperation than one developed without their contribution. This process can take some time, particularly if the implications of the measures and objectives are discussed thoroughly.

The responsibilities for establishing a system for monitoring effectiveness and for collecting and analyzing the data might best be lodged in an office of "research and evaluation" or "planning" which, in many state corrections agencies, has a performance-monitoring role and a research and statistics capability.

2. Assess Currently Available Data.

Many of the measures rely on information available in one form or another at the agency level or at the individual institution level. Considerable effort may be required to determine the specific nature and quality of the data, such as variability in definitions or reporting procedures among various units and information on the validity of the information (Are all events counted? Are the counts accurate? And so forth.).

3. Establish Periodic Data-Reporting Procedures

This step might involve promulgation of definitions and criteria, establishment of procedures for collecting data, and establishment of report forms and instructions for their completion, or modification of existing forms. This procedure can become complex for measures involving the selection of a random sample of offenders.

4. Modify Data-Processing Procedures

Modification can include new or revised coding for additional data, programming for the necessary data processing, and developing new output formats and reports. Some of the programming can be relatively simple, such as for calculating average daily population; it can become complex for calculating parole revocation measures (Measure 8c) and changes in attitude ratings of groups of inmates (Measure 7).

5. Review the Procedures with Prison and Parole Officials for Meaningfulness and for Operational Feasibility; Test the Measures

The procedure for collecting information for even the most seemingly ''simple'' measures can become appallingly detailed to cover all contingencies. For a complex measure such as physical examination, detailed procedures are very important. Close reviews by officials with operations responsibility and a test of the procedures—in terms of both the ease of collection and the accuracy of the data collected—appear highly desirable before regular measuring gets underway.

6. Establish a Schedule for the Collection and Reporting of Data from Line Units

Once the procedures for collecting data have been developed and tested for accuracy, the system can be put into operation. Schedules for providing data should be established for regular reporting.

COSTS AND STAFF NEEDED FOR A PERFORMANCE-MONITORING EFFORT: PRELIMINARY ESTIMATES

The effort required to implement a full performance-monitoring capability as described in Chapters II and III appears to be substantial. Those chapters provide some rough estimates of the amount of effort required to implement some of the measures. On the basis of the limited experience in North Carolina in developing and testing a few of the measurement concepts for this project, a minimum of two to three person-years of research-evaluation staff time would appear necessary to carry out steps 1 through 6 above for all of the measures except for the measure of physical health, which would require more effort, most likely by the state department of health. Officials with operational responsibility in the prison and parole systems would also have to spend large amounts of time working with those persons charged with developing the detailed data-collection procedures.

The continuing costs for regularly collecting and analyzing the monitoring data once steps 1 through 6 above have been accomplished will vary greatly according to the size of the corrections agency (number of facilities as well as the number of inmates and parolees), the number of measures implemented, existing data-collection and reporting procedures (if they can be modified or expanded slightly to include the data for monitoring effectiveness), and the extent of automated record keeping and data processing. One to two persons full time in a central evaluation/analytic research staff would seem to be required. Additional support from the state department of health probably would be necessary for sanitation inspections and for physical examinations of inmates. The only major cash outlay (other than for salaries) would be for the physical examinations of inmates—approximately $100 per exam or between $20,000 and $75,000 each time inmate health is monitored.

APPENDIX A

OTHER AREAS IN WHICH MEASUREMENT IS NEEDED

There are other areas in which measurement and annual monitoring seem desirable, either because of major effort on the part of corrections agencies to change conditions or because of a belief that these conditions affect criminality or positive reintegration into the community. This project has concentrated on practical measures for certain aspects of rehabilitation and incarceration which could be developed with relatively modest effort. But additional research seems desirable in three other areas:

1. Measurement of social adjustment and social functioning
2. Measurement of deterrence and crime prevention
3. Additional measurements for humane treatment.

This section discusses some of the measurement issues and provides suggestions for additional research.

Social Adjustment and Social Functioning

Corrections services, particularly during parole, are often concerned with enhancing the social well-being of offenders—the ability of the offenders to cope with their personal problems which might have contributed to their original criminal involvement and which, if not corrected, might lead to renewed criminality, might require intervention by welfare personnel

on behalf of the offenders or their families, or might seriously affect or limit the positive integration/reintegration into society.

Aspects of concern may include:

- *Family functioning problems;* instability of living arrangement or home environment; marital or general family adjustment problems which create difficulties the client cannot handle or which require welfare intervention because of the client's neglect and failure to meet responsibilities. Although a majority of released offenders are estimated to be unattached males with no family responsibilities, the remainder of the releasees would be candidates for this type of service.
- *Financial management problems,* which threaten family stability or employment or may lead to further criminal activities.
- *Illiteracy* or other education/intelligence handicaps and limitations affecting the client's ability to function or to be self-supporting by legitimate means.
- *Extensive association with and influence by others with criminal involvement* or related problems; a strong tendency to be led by more sophisticated criminal or delinquent associates.
- *Poor sociability,* social relationships are generally unsatisfactory, limited in number, or of poor quality.

Measurement of changes in social functioning and social adjustment seems hampered by several conditions:

- *Lack of testing instruments.* There appear to be no tested, reliable scales for measuring social functioning of offenders nor scales for other social services that could be readily transferred.
- *Need to avoid "middle class" value judgments.* The development of such measures has to avoid reflecting middle-class biases or value judgments that might not be meaningful in the offender's society.
- *Difficulties in data collection.* Because the reliability of responses from the offender is often questionable, observation of the family and collection of information from different sources would probably be required; hence the measurement effort would be very time-consuming.
- *Problems in choosing aspects to measure.* It is not clear what aspects of social functioning should have the highest priority for measurement—or which ones occur most frequently and have the greatest impact on offender well-being.

Some special program evaluations have attempted to measure the effects of various corrections strategies on social functioning and community adjustment. They have used such measures as quality of marital and other family relationships, quality of friendships, church attendance and participation in various organized community activities, self-perception, and social functioning.[1] There are some state correctional activities underway concerned with measuring social adjustment, and some literature exists in the field of evaluation of social services and changes in social functioning which could be used in developing measurement.

In New York State, the supervising parole officer of each offender assesses the individual's social adjustment at the time of release from parole or return to an institution and gives one of three ratings:

1. *Definitely better* than when the offender was committed
2. *Little change* since being committed
3. *Definitely worse* since being committed.

The criteria for making the ratings are somewhat unclear. Instruction to the parole officer provided by the New York State Corrections Agency is shown in exhibit A-1.

A basic measurement concept could be the percentage-point change in offenders (from intake to discharge from parole) with one or more severe problems of social functioning. By using casework records to compare the social adjustment of a sample of offenders at intake into corrections custody with their adjustment at conclusion of parole, statistics could be developed to indicate the extent to which corrections is overcoming major problems of social functioning. The ratings could be made by the parole officer, but they might have more credibility if made by a special observer.

To achieve reliable, meaningful statistics, some type of grading or rating of social conditions and clear guidelines on what constitutes a "severe" problem seems needed. A possible guideline is "a problem which, if not corrected, appears likely to lead to continued criminal activity or which will seriously limit the offender's ability to manage his own affairs." The guidelines should be specific enough that different parole officers making independent judgments of the same case generally would arrive at the same diagnosis. Because these will be professional judgments, some variability is likely to occur no matter how explicit the guidelines; but without guidelines and some scale, the variability is likely to be so great that the comparison of ratings is meaningless. A distinction probably needs to be made between those clients with "major and basic problems" which are correctable or which can be alleviated with social services administered by or through the correction agency ("influenceable" by corrections) and those which are not correctable (not influenceable) by the corrections agency because they stem from permanent mental, physical, or character impairments and disorders.

Some work has been done on ways to classify individuals objectively to facilitate determination of changes in their conditions which might be attributable to the services provided by corrections (or any other social service agency). Research on evaluation of social services, which is being conducted in another part of this broad project, has uncovered an approach used by Resources Management Corporation and Duke University to develop (under a U.S. Department of Health, Education and Welfare—Social and Rehabilitative Service grant) a Multi-Dimensional Functional Assessment Scale. The project has identified five major dimensions of human functioning:

1. Physical health
2. Mental health
3. Social resources
4. Economic resources
5. Capacity for daily living

Trained interviewers (not clinicians) administer a 75-minute questionnaire to the client, gather any other factual, observable data, and use their perceptions to make a "summary judgment" on each of the five di-

---

1. See Lipton, Martinson, and Wilk, *The Effectiveness of Correctional Treatment,* pp. 448–512.

PROCEDURE FOLLOWED BY PAROLE OFFICERS
IN EVALUATING PAROLEE'S SOCIAL ADJUSTMENT

Effective January 1, 1962, the following codes are to be used only at the termination of parole which occurs by discharge from parole supervision because of expiration of maximum sentence or because of any other reason or by return to the institution as a parole violator.

	Codes For Social Adjustment on Parole As Compared to That Prior to Conviction		
Conformance with Rules and Regulations of Parole	Definitely Better	Little Change	Definitely Worse
No violations	A	B	C
One or more technical violations	D	E	F
One or more new arrests without conviction	G	H	I
Various court adjudications	J	K	L
One or more convictions of offense less than misdemeanor	M	N	O
One or more convictions of misdemeanor	P	Q	R
One or more convictions of felony	S	T	U

As indicated above the Parole Officer supervising a caseload will only be required to choose one letter for evaluating the parolee's social adjustment. It will be the Parole Officer's professional judgment which will be used in deciding whether a parolee's social adjustment on parole was definitely better, definitely worse, or little different than his social adjustment before commitment. For example, a parolee returned as a technical parole violator may be considered to have improved under parole supervision if his employment record was definitely better than it was before commitment. Also, it is conceivable, although unlikely, that a parolee without any violations may be considered to have made a worse adjustment. Obviously there are no hard and fast rules that can be applied to making such an evaluation. Each parolee presents an individual situation and in the final analysis it is the Parole Officer's professional judgment which places the parolee in any one of the three groups. When there is doubt as to improvement or deterioration, the category Little Change would be the one to employ.

The Parole Officer will designate at the time of parole termination the parolee's adjustment on the Monthly Supervision Report in the Change of Status column by placing the appropriate code letter in a circle. The code letter is to be entered only when an individual's parole terminates by Discharge by Maximum Expiration of Sentence, Court Order, Death, Other Reasons, or by Return to the institution as a parole violator.

SOURCE: New York State Department of Corrections.

mensions. The judgment consists of the following ratings:

1. Outstanding
2. O.K., average
3. Mild impairment
4. Moderate impairment
5. Severe impairment
6. Complete impairment

An example of ratings in the area of social resources which might be adapted for measuring social functioning for released offenders is shown in exhibit A-2. This form probably contains more rating categories than necessary.

Characteristics that could be examined to develop an index of family functioning have been identified in the St. Paul Scale of Family Functioning and discussed in a book titled *Family and Community Functioning.*[2] A seven-part rating scale from adequate to marginal to inadequate (justifying public intervention) was developed to measure various aspects of

- General family functioning
- Family relationships and unity

---

2. Ludwig L. Geismar, *Family and Community Functioning.*

- Individual behavior and adjustment
- Social activities

The example of the criteria for the ratings is shown in exhibit A-3.

A similar approach is suggested for corrections, with guidelines clearly identified for a parole officer or other person collecting the information from interviews with the offender, family, social service workers or others, as appropriate. The ratings would be used to classify the offender's condition—perhaps on a scale of 1 (adequate) to 4 (severe impairment) for each of the following indices:

- Family functioning
- Financial management
- Educational or intellectual handicaps
- Association with and influence by undesirables
- General sociability

Other research might prove applicable. In 1976, the Illinois Department of Corrections was developing an extensive performance information system. The department and the contractor seek to report objectively on family functioning and to establish methods for using the information. At this writing, there were no reports indicating the specific measures and data-col-

Exhibit A-3
CRITERIA FOR RATING FAMILY FUNCTIONING

Inadequate: Functioning Harmful to the Point Where Community Has a Right to Intervene	Marginal: Functioning Not Sufficiently Harmful to Justify Intervention	Adequate: Functioning is in Line with Community Expectations
Laws and/or mores are clearly violated. Behavior of family members is a threat to the community.	Major laws are not being violated, although behavior of family members is at variance with status group expectations.	Laws are obeyed and mores observed. Behavior is in line with status group expectations.
Family life is characterized by extreme conflict, neglect, severe deprivation, unhappiness or very poor relationships resulting in physical and/or emotional suffering of family members; disruption of family life is imminent; children are in clear and present danger because of above conditions or other behavior inimical to their welfare.	Family life is generally marked by conflict, apathy, or unstable relationships which can be seen as a potential threat to the family's and/or the community's welfare. Family is poorly equipped to deal with problems; family members are frequently dissatisfied with their condition and do not possess the knowledge or ability to improve it. Although children are not being properly socialized and their environment is not fully conducive to healthy physical or emotional development, they are not in imminent danger.	Family members are generally satisfied with their lot, and their needs are being met. Efforts aimed at improvement are made where appropriate. Family life is stable; members have a sense of belonging and sharing mutually compatible goals and expectations. Problems are faced and dealt with appropriately. Children are being raised in an atmosphere conducive to healthy growth and development. Socialization process stresses positive mental health, preparation for present and future roles and the acquisition of social skills.

SOURCE: Ludwig L. Geismar, *Family and Community Functioning.*

lection procedures to be used. The Bureau of Probation and Parole in the Wisconsin Division of Corrections has developed a check list to indicate the presence of problems of social functioning; this list would be used for diagnosing the social service needs of offenders and it could be used to check off conditions when leaving parole. There were no specific guidelines as to what constituted a problem. The criteria assessed are shown in exhibit A-4.

Deterrence and Crime Prevention

A frequently stated objective of corrections and incarceration in particular is to deter (discourage) and to prevent crime. Incarceration potentially does this through (1) locking up offenders likely to continue criminal actions so that they cannot commit further crime against the public and (2) deterring other persons from committing offenses because of the threat of incarceration.

There have been a number of analyses to try to determine the deterrent effects of incarceration on crime.[3] The general conclusion, though still controversial, appears to be that severe sentences have a deterrent effect, at least for the offense of murder, but that the certainty of punishment—the likelihood of being apprehended and convicted—appears to be the chief deterrent for most crimes. An analysis could be conducted to estimate the deterrent effect of incarceration on crime in a state which had enough reported crimes and convictions for the statistical analysis. However, this deterrent effect does not appear to be worth an annual monitoring effort by corrections personnel when one considers the fact that the length of sentence, compared with the likelihood of apprehension, has relatively little impact on reported crime rates, and the fact that correctional authorities probably have little to do with the length of time served (other than perhaps to control the date of parole). The deterrent effect might be more suitable for a special study conducted every five or ten years to determine trends over time.

___

3. W. C. Bailey, J. D. Martin, and L. N. Gray, in "Crime and Deterrence," *Journal of Research in Crime and Delinquency,* vol. 11, no. 2, July 1974, pp. 124–143, make an analysis of these effects as well as providing an extensive set of references. James Q. Wilson

also discusses the deterrent effect in "If Every Criminal Knew He Would Be Punished if Caught. . .," *New York Times Magazine,* January 28, 1973, p. 9. A general discussion of the deterrent effects of punishment is provided by Johannes Andenaes, "The General Preventive Effects of Punishment," *University of Pennsylvania Law Review,* vol. 114, no. 7, May 1966. Also, George E. Antunes and A. Lee Hunt report on "The Impact of Certainty and Severity of Punishment on Levels of Crime in American States."

Exhibit A-4
WISCONSIN DIVISION OF CORRECTIONS—CLIENT PROFILE CHECK LIST

BUREAU OF PROBATION AND PAROLE
Client Profile Check List For _____
Name of Client

Explanation of Categories
STRENGTH: (An item that might exert a positive influence on the client's adjustment.)
NEUTRAL:　 (An item that is not related to the case, not applicable or unknown.)
PROBLEM:　 (An item that might exert a negative influence on the client's adjustment.)

The significant information necessary to complete this *Check List* should be available from the Social History or Preparole investigation. Consider carefully all of these items below (they follow the general sequence of the Social History Investigation Outline) and check those which should be considered in the case supervision planning for this client.

STRENGTH	NEUTRAL	PROBLEM	
			1. Use of Aliases
			2. Appearance
			3. Area of Residence
			4. Court-ordered Conditions/Obligations
			5. Prior Record
			6. Relationship with Parents
			7. Marital History of Parents
			8. Relationship with Other Family Members
			9. Family Criminal History
			10. Client Sexual Behavior
			11. Educational Attainment
			12. School Adjustment
			13. Abuse of Drugs/Alcohol
			14. Physical Health
			15. Emotional Stability
			16. Financial Management—Debts
			17. Present Job Adjustment
			18. Employment History
			19. Marketable Skills
			20. Use of Leisure Time
			21. Associates/Companions
			22. Attitude of Spouse
			23. Relationship with Spouse
			24. Marital History of Client
			25. Present Marital Status of Client
			26. Emotional Climate of Home
			27. Community Acceptance
			28. Ability to Communicate
			29. Self-Concept
			30. Acceptance of Responsibility
			31. Response to Supervision
			32. Previous Performance on Supervision
			33. Motivation to Change
			34. Relationships with Police
			35. Resource Availability
			36. Gang Involvement
			37. Absconder—Risk
			38. Crime Against Person—Risk
			39. Crime Against Property—Risk
			40. Other

At best, this type of analysis gives only a crude indication of the deterrent effects of incarceration. Morris and Zimring appear to be correct in stating that

> historical, comparative and survey methods can all throw light on our central question (deterrence and corrections); but the incisive beam is likely to come only from the field experiment. Here, as elsewhere in criminology, the field experiment which is designed deliberately to test the consequences of increased or reduced severity of a punishment for a given type of human behavior has substantial political obstacles to its acceptance and implementation.[4]

How much crime is prevented by incarcerating offenders who would otherwise be committing further offenses? It is impossible to estimate accurately the types and amounts of crime locked-up offenders might be committing if they were free. Hence, this type of analysis is not recommended for annual monitoring. The obvious inability of offenders to commit crimes against the public while they are in prison has been an argument for justifying long prison sentences for repeat offenders.[5] Yet it can be argued, too, that prolonged incarceration is counterproductive and may stimulate inmates, on completion of their sentences, to commit more crimes than they would have if they had been released earlier.

Additional Measurements for Humane Treatment

Humane treatment, of course, involves much more than providing sanitary facilities, health care, and protection from other inmates discussed in Chapter II. It encompasses adequate food and clothing and provision of certain basic civil rights—access to courts and legal services, access to some grievance procedures, mail service. No specific measurements for these aspects of humane treatment were suggested in Chapter II for two reasons: it is difficult to monitor systematically the extent that civil rights are provided or improperly curtailed; and second, the possible, additional measures seemed to have much less validity or less importance than the other measures suggested. However, several possibilities for monitoring might be developed.

A relatively simple approach taken by states with formal grievance procedures is to monitor the *number of grievances, by type, total, and total divided by the average daily population*. This measure seems to have relatively little validity. The numbers of complaints by type are difficult to relate to the extent of conditions: inmates might be reluctant to complain, they might be hindered from filing grievances, they might submit large numbers of unjustified complaints to cause difficulty for the corrections agency processing the complaints, the complaints might not reach the corrections headquarters, or they might not be formally filed because of remedial actions at the facility level. For states with a process of hearings and verification of grievances, the data could be presented best in terms of *the number of verified or justified grievances, by type, total, and total divided by ADP*.

Certain aspects of food quality can be monitored relatively easily. The Food and Nutrition Board of the National Academy of Sciences has established guidelines on recommended daily dietary allowances for adult males, adult females, and youths. A possible measure is the estimated *percentage of meals that meet minimum dietetic standards for food value and balance*. Officials could estimate the percentage by making unannounced site visits to facilities at meal times, perhaps as a part of a sanitation inspection. They could actually weigh the portions of food served and, using tables with caloric values for various types of foods, determine if the meals meet minimum standards. It is possible that minimum standards for caloric value will be met while there are shortages of meat, citrus fruits, or milk products; deficiencies would need to be noted.

Another approach, considerably less reliable, is to compare the amount of food—by type—allocated to the facility with the number of inmates to be served. Because of spoilage, thefts, and other food losses, the amount of food actually served to inmates will at times be below that planned, and possibly below minimum health standards.

Measures of caloric value and balance do not cover taste, heat, appearance, and variety of food served, which are also important. Outsiders—possibly a panel of food experts—could arrive unannounced several times a year to eat regular institutional meals and to rate their quality.[6] Surveying inmates with regard to variety, taste, and attractiveness does not appear to be reliable, because over time, virtually any

---

4. Norval Morris and Frank Zimring, "Deterrence and Correction," *The Annals of the American Academy of Political and Social Science*, vol. 381, January 1969.

5. This idea is discussed by James Q. Wilson in "Lock 'Em Up and Other Thoughts on Crime," *New York Times Magazine*, March 9, 1975.

6. Donald Dresden, food critic, rated the food at one facility of the D.C. Correctional Complex, "Dining in the D.C. Jail," *The Washington* (D.C.) *Post, Potomac*, June 17, 1973.

type of institutional food will lose its appeal and apparent quality to the residents.[7]

Reid Montgomery has developed and tested a survey approach to examining a number of aspects of humane treatment, including food, legal access, medical services, privacy, and visitation in South Carolina.[8] The survey was administered only to persons being discharged from incarceration. As discussed earlier, there is considerable doubt about the credibility of inmate responses to a survey on controversial issues; inmates clearly sense whether their responses make a prison "look good" or "look bad" and it is difficult to validate some of them. Still, this departure survey could be administered with relatively little effort, and would obtain opinions with regard to food, sanitation conditions, and clothing.

Much research needs to be done, in fact, to determine if an inmate survey of prison conditions can be developed which would produce findings that can be validated. If a valid survey can be developed, it could be administered to (1) a sample of as few as 100 to 200 randomly selected offenders in or being released from all facilities in the corrections system, (2) to samples of 100 offenders in or being released from each major facility, or (3) to all literate inmates being discharged.

There are other aspects of humane or possibly inhumane treatment for which no tentative measurement procedures are presented. These include brutality or alleged brutality of prison officials, clean linen or clothing, recreational hours and facilities, library facilities, educational or vocational educational opportunities, meaningful and safe work opportunities, access to grievance mechanisms and to courts, and due process for punishment. Many of these could be included as topics in a survey of inmates. If inmates identify any of these as severe problems, perhaps they could become topics for special studies.

---

7. The quality of prison food was assessed in the Michigan health care evaluation by a questionnaire administered to the sample of 458 inmates. Inmates were asked to rate the adequacy ("adequate," "somewhat adequate," "grossly inadequate") of the balance of the diet, quality of food preparation, amount, and cleanliness.

8. Reid Montgomery, "A Measurement of Inmate Satisfaction/Dissatisfaction in Selected South Carolina Institutions." The survey was not being used by the South Carolina Department of Corrections as of 1976.

APPENDIX B

EXPERIENCE WITH THE EFFECTIVENESS MEASUREMENT PROJECT IN NORTH CAROLINA

The Urban Institue and the Office of State Budget in the Department of Administration of the State of North Carolina began this joint study to develop and institute procedures for measuring the effectiveness of various state services in early 1975. In March 1975, corrections was selected as one of the services to be included in the effort, and the North Carolina Department of Correction became a participant in the project. The Urban Institute was designated to provide the original framework for such a study by providing an extensive set of possible corrections measures based on information received from other state corrections agencies and a review of numerous research and evaluation efforts. In June 1975, a catalogue of candidate measures, data-collection procedures, and other pertinent descriptive information were delivered to North Carolina officials for refinement and tailoring to North Carolina. The original list covered concerns ranging from quality of services to the inmates to deterrence of crime against the public.

The measures suggested were revised at length, first, by personnel from The Urban Institute and the budget and planning divisions of the North Carolina

Department of Administration, and second, by personnel from these agencies and from the Research and Evaluation Office of the state's Department of Correction. Each review not only provided additions, deletions, and modifications to the set of measures, but also preliminary investigations into the existence, availability, and form of the data needed in the North Carolina system. This revision process took several person-months, and produced a list of measures (see exhibit B-1) which was circulated among all division heads within the Department of Correction for their comment. Several other related agencies in the state were invited to contribute—the Department of Natural Resources, Division of Community Assistance—Law and Order, the Department of Human Resources, Division of Youth Services (which had been separated recently from the Department of Correction and now maintains jurisdiction over all youths committed to Youth Development Schools). Youth Services elected not to be involved in the measurement project.

Personal follow-up with Division of Prisons' personnel provided valuable information regarding the desirability and feasibility of the development of each measure. Revisions continued to be made at each level of contact with agency personnel, especially in the procedures for collecting data. In many instances, the

This appendix was prepared by Karan Bunn, North Carolina Office of State Budget.

Exhibit B-1

CRITERIA FOR ASSESSING MEASURES

H—High
M—Medium
L—Low
NI—Not an Issue

Subject of Measure of Effectiveness	Uniqueness (Related Measure No.)	Precision	Validity	Controllability	Timeliness	Privacy	Cost to Collect	Overall Importance	Preliminary Priority Weighting
A.1. No. of Escapes	H	H	H	H	H	NI	L	H	10
A.2. % Recaptured	H	M	H	M-L	H-M	NI	L	M-L	3
A.3. No. of Crimes, Escapees	H	H	M-L	M-H	M	NI	L	M	5
A.4. No. of Crimes, W.R.	H	H	M-L	M-H	M	NI	L	M	5
A.5. No. of Escape Attempts	M(A.1)	L	H	L	H	NI	L	M-L	3
A.6. Contraband	M-L(A.7,9,14)	H	L-M	L-M	H	NI	L	L	1
A.7. Contraband Stopped	M-L(A.6-8,14)	H	L	L-M	H	NI	L	L	1
A.8. Contraband Incidents	M-L(A.6,8,9,14)	M-H	M	L-M	H-M	NI	L	L	1
A.9. Drugs in Urine	M(A.7-9,14)	H-M	H	L-M	H	Yes	M	M-H	5
A.10. Guard Assaults	M-H(A.11)	H	H	M	H	NI	L	M	5
A.11. Perceptions of Security	M(A.10)	H	M	M	M	NI	L-M	L-M	2
A.12. Inmate Assaults	M-H(A.13)	M	M	L-M	H	No	L	M	5
A.13. Inmate Victimization	M(A.12)	L	H	L-M	H	No	L-M	M	4
A.14. Inmate Fears	H	L	H	L-M	M	No	L-M	L	0
A.15. Suicides	M(B.32)	M-H	H	L-M	M-L	NI	L	M	5
A.16. Self-Inflicted Injuries	M(A.15)	L-M	M	L-M	H-M	NI	L	L-M	3
A.17. Disciplinary Actions	H	M	H	M	H	NI	L	M-H	7
A.18. Promotions/Demotions	M-H(A.17)	M-H	M	M	M	NI	L	M	5
A.19. Incidents of Unrest	H	H	H	M	M	NI	L	M-H	7
A.20. Overcrowding, Inmate Days	M(A.21)	H	H	H	H	NI	L	H	9
A.21. Percent over Capacity	M(A.20)	H	H	H	H	NI	L	M-H	7
A.22. Sanitation Rating	H	H	M-H	M-H	H	NI	H	M-H	3
A.23. Inadequate Temperature Control	H	M	M	M-H	H	NI	M	L-M	1
A.24. Plumbing Adequacy	L-M(A.21)	M	H	M-H	H	NI	M	L	1
A.25. Diet Adequacy	H	M	M-H	H	H	NI	L-M	M	4

Measure									
A.26. Food Quality	H	H	M	H	H	NI	L	L-M	3
A.27. Clothing Adequacy	H	M-H	H	H	H	NI	M	L-M	1
A.28. Guard Brutality	H	L	H	H	H-M	No	H	M	1
A.29. Percent Needing Medical Care	H	M	H	M	H	Yes	M-H	H	6
A.30. Disease Rates	H	M	H	M	M-L	Yes	L	M-H	7
A.31. Speed of Care	H	L-M	M	M-H	H	Yes	M	L-M	1
A.32. Inmate Rating of Medical Care	M(A.29)	L-M	M-H	L-M	H	Yes	L	L	1
A.33. Waiting Time for Treatment	H	M	M	H	H	NI	L	L-M	3
A.34. Percent Needing Dental Care	H	M	H	H	H	NI	M-H	M	2
A.35. Medical Cures	M(A.29)	H	M	H	H-M	Yes	M-H	H	6
A.36. Injuries	M(A.37)	M	M	M	M	NI	L	M	5
A.37. Job Illnesses	M(A.37)	M-L	H	M	M-L	NI	L-M	L-M	2
A.38. Mental Health	M(A.38)	M-H	H	H?	H	Yes	H	H	5
A.39. M.H. Needs Met	M(A.39)	M	H	H	H	Yes	H	H	5
A.40. Mental Illness	M(A.39)	M	M-H	L-M	M-L	Yes	L-M	H	8
A.41. Change in Mental Health	M(A.39)	H	M	L-M	M-L	Yes	M-H	H	6
A.42. Parole Success	H	H	M-H	L-M	M	NI	L	H	9
A.43. Probation Success	H	H	M-H	L-M	M	NI	L	H	9
B.1. Recidivism	H	M?	M-H	L	L	NI	M	H	7
B.2. Time to Reconviction	M(A.42,43;B.1)	H	M-H	L	L	NI	L	M	5
B.3. Prev. Incarceration	M(B.1)	H	M	L	L	NI	L	M	5
B.4. No. Prev. Incn.	H	M	M	L	L	NI	L	M	5
B.5. No. Convictions	M(B.4)	M	M	L	L	NI	L	M-L	3
B.6. Years Incarc.	H	M	M	L	L	NI	L	M-L	3
B.7. Occupation	M(B.10)	M-L	M-H	L-M	M-L	No	H	M	1
B.8. Employment	M(B.10)	M-L	M-H	L-M	M-L	No	H	M-H	3
B.9. Steady Employ.	M(B.10)	M-L	M	L	M-L	No	H	M	1
B.10. Income	M(B.8)	L	M	L-M	M-L	No	H	M	1
B.11. Voc. Ed. Participation	M(B.7)	M	M	M	H	NI	L-M	L-M	2
B.12. Comp. Voc. Ed.	L(B.7,11)	H	L-M	L-M	M	NI	L	L	1
B.13. Percent Placed	H	M	H	M	M	NI	L	M	5
B.14. Work Release Success	H	H	M	M	M	NI	L	M	5
B.15. No. Participating in W.R.	M(B.14)	M	M	M	M	NI	M	M	3
B.16. Part. Rating of W.R.	M(B.13,14)	M-L	M-H	M	L-M	No	M-H	M	2
B.17. Educational Advancement	H	M-H	M	M	M	Yes	L-M	M-L	2
B.18. Percent Illiterate	M(B.17)	M-H	M	H	M	Yes	L-M	M	4
B.19. Mental Retard.	M(B.17,18)	M-H	M-L	L	H	Yes	L-M	M	4
B.20. Continue Voc. Ed.	H	M-L	M	L-M	L-M	No	H	M	1
B.21. High School Diplomas Awarded	M(B.17)	H	M	M	M	NI	L	M-L	3

Exhibit B-1 (continued)

CRITERIA FOR ASSESSING MEASURES

H–High
M–Medium
L–Low
NI–Not an Issue

Subject of Measure of Effectiveness	Uniqueness (Related Measure No.)	Precision	Validity	Controllability	Timeliness	Privacy	Cost to Collect	Overall Importance	Preliminary Priority Weighting
B.22. Family Visits	H	H	L	L	H	NI	L	L	1
B.23. Meeting Family Responsibility	H	M-L	H	L-M	L	No	H	M-H	3
B.24. Undesirable Associates	H	H	L-M	L-M	M-L	NI	L	M-L	3
B.25. Meeting Financial Needs	M(B.23)	L-M	M-H	L	L	No	H	M	1
B.26. Residential Stability	M(B.23)	M-L	M-L	L	L	No	M-H	M-L	0
B.27. Community Participation	H	M	M	L	L	No	H	M	1
B.28. Drug/Alcohol Use	M(A.42,43;B.1)	H	M	L	L	NI	L	M	5
B.29. Perceived Safety	H	H	M	L-M	M-L	NI	M	L	1
B.30. Parole Length	H	H	M-L	M	M	NI	L	L-M	3
B.31. % Probation Served	H	H	M-H	M	M	NI	L	M	5
B.32. Deaths	M(A.15)	H	H	L	H	NI	NX	M-H	8
B.33. Participants' Rating of Program	M(B.16,34)	L-M	M-H	M	L-M	NI	M	M	3
B.34. Rating Usefulness	M(B.16,33)	L-M	M-H	M	L-M	NI	M	M	3
B.35. Program Placements	M(B.33,34)	H	M	M-H	H	NI	M	L	
B.36. Percent Participating	H	H	M	L-M	H	NI	M	L-M	1
B.37. No. Grievances	H	H	M-H	L-M	M-H	NI	L	H	9
B.38. Vandalism	H	M	H	L-M	H	NI	L	M	5
C.1. Length of Time Served	H	H	M-L	M	L	NI	L	M	5
D.1. Change in Crime	H	L	H	L?	L	NI	H	H	5

more thoroughly a measure was investigated, the less it appeared likely that such a measure as proposed could be instituted. The North Carolina Department of Correction's computer contained a substantial amount of information in the Inmates' Record File; but the organization of the data made computer runs costly. Once the current project to automate offender records is completed, information should prove more accessible. Programming assistance was not readily available during the study period because the data-processing staff was occupied with the installation of the computer.

Because of the large number of measures considered for selection, some system for establishing priorities was needed. The Urban Institute developed a rating scheme to assess the important aspects of a measure (see Chapter I and exhibit 2). These included uniqueness, precision, validity, controllability, timeliness, and privacy. Ratings were assigned to each measure for each of these criteria; these ratings ranged from high to low, taking an appropriate value from 5 to 1(H=5, M−H=4, M=3, M−L=2, L=1). In addition to these basic criteria, the overall importance of the measure and cost to collect were assessed. The worth of the measure was assessed in relationship to its importance to the Department of Correction for evaluating programs, for requesting funds from the legislature, for accounting to the public, and so forth. And a subjective rating of its overall quality—based on the previously discussed criteria—was made. The cost was estimated within the range of 5 to 0, with 0 implying no cost. The priority list was developed by doubling the importance value and subtracting the cost rating (the importance of the measure was judged to be considerably more important than the cost).

Measures were then ranked in priority order. Measures within the same priority rating (i.e., all the 10's) were ranked strictly according to judgment. If, when a higher priority measure was developed, it was found possible to generate a lower priority item with little or no additional effort, the latter was included with the higher priority measure. Because of the Department of Correction's interest in certain areas regardless of the resources required, several items with a low "preliminary priority rating" (they had been considered highly important but very costly) were given higher priority ratings. These items included measures on employment and family responsibility. The top nineteen priorities (including thirty-two measures) were selected for development, with highest importance attached to measures of incarceration services.

The resulting priority measures were grouped according to the types of data-collection procedures needed (special collection procedures, existing data, and so forth) and, according to the nature of the measure (health, recidivism, and so forth), assigned to various team members for further investigation and documentation. Areas and topics to be covered were as follows:

Order of Final Priority	Measure	Identification on Exhibit B.1
1	Escapes	A.1
2	Overcrowding	A.20, 21
3	Recidivism	B.1, 2, 3; A.42, 43
4	Mental illness	A.38, 39, 40, 41
5	Deaths, suicides	A.15; B.32
6	Employment	B.8
7	Disciplinary actions, contraband	A.17, 18
8	Diseases	A.30
9	Incidents of unrest	A.19
10	Sanitation conditions	A.22
11	Meeting family responsibilities	B.23
12	Medical care	A.29, 35
13	Job placement	B.13
14	Inmate grievances	B.37
15	Number of crimes while on escape/ authorized leave	A.3, 4
16	Inmate assaults	A.12
17	Promotion and demotion	A.18
18	Urinalysis exam	A.9
19	Injuries	A.36

Once these priorities had been developed, the team set about implementing as many of the measures on incarceration as possible. Highest attention was given to the measures with priorities of 1 to 5 and 7 to 9. The problems encountered were typical of any practical application of theoretical concepts. The introduction of new approaches into all established organizations provides opportunities for bureaucratic inertia to display itself. In the case of the North Carolina Department of Correction, an additional problem was evident: the expanding inmate population, unaccompanied by an increase in staff, was straining the limits of the existing workloads. It was essential, therefore, to provide administrative personnel with strong justification for the goals of the project and to limit sharply its intrusion into the daily activities of the department.

The key concept—that of measuring the performance of the department's activities—already had been accepted in principle as a result of two developments. First, the requirements for obtaining federal funds through the Law Enforcement Assistance Administration included an evaluation phase on each project for which money was requested; the evaluation was to determine whether the stated objectives of the project had been achieved. Second, the department had a "management-by-objective" system which required administrators to develop measurable goals, along with procedures for data-gathering and analysis, for every program, regardless of the funding source. Despite the conviction of top department officials of the necessity of evaluation, inertia as well as the size and diversity of the department contributed to the difficulty of gathering data for monitoring. North Carolina has 77 units housing inmates. These range in size from large institutions (up to 1,200 inmates) to field units (100 inmates) and are spread geographically throughout the state. The differences in administering such units led to the gathering of quite different types of data, because definitions of data required varied from place to place. Existing reports from units in the field to the central command also reflect this diversity.

The very nature of the administrative structure of the department further encouraged a diversity of reporting schemes. The units were classified into three categories: Institutions, the six, large, high-security prisons; Youth Complex, facilities housing youthful offenders; and, the Geographic Command, responsible for the minimum security field units. (This last was further divided into six geographic areas, with each unit reporting to its respective area administrator.) Each area had adequate incident-reporting practices for the control of the type of problems predominant within its area, but, from a central viewpoint, such independence posed problems in reporting directly comparable information for specific kinds of activities.

As an example of the methods necessary to provide some consistency in the nature of data being gathered for Measure 3 (incidents of failure of internal security), a new data-collection instrument was devised (shown in exhibit 4 in Chapter II). Design considerations in developing the form led to the following features:

1. A single form was devised for reporting any one of the four types of incidents. This form reduced the problem of paper proliferation.
2. Information was requested in its simplest form, as a check in the appropriate block or as a blank to be filled in. This report is simply a device to count the numbers of incidents occurring, without considering the management action which may stem from the details of a specific incident. Because little time was required to complete the form, objections from the field that these reports duplicated incident reporting were minimized.
3. All instructions for completing the form were printed on the form itself. This eased the task of data submission and improved the general quality of responses.
4. The request for data among the four incident types was standarized.

Several meetings were held with institution superintendents and area administrators to explain the purposes and nature of the report and the procedures for completing a report before it was introduced. After a delay of several months, reporting began in mid-July 1976. Six weeks after implementation, some units apparently were not using the reporting form, and other sources were cross-checked to identify lapses in the reporting system.

Difficulties with the computer system and delays in arranging the schedules (transportation of inmates, marshalling medical services, and so forth), prevented the implementation of the measures for physical health and attitudinal changes (Measures 6 and 7) during the lifetime of the joint Urban Institute—State of North Carolina Project. Because of centralization and control of the examination procedures, however, these measures would not have the inherent problems of geographic definition found in Measure 3.

The experience with corrections monitoring in North Carolina indicated that implementing a monitoring capability on a department level generally will require:

- Finding a team of interested persons with at least a year's time to work on the development and implementation of the measure.
- Overcoming both general inertia and specific objections of program managers. To accomplish this goal, top officials will have to make a strong commitment to the project and give it high priority, and additional resources will have to be found. Moreover, the project not only must minimize inconvenience to program managers, but it also must involve them in developing measures and data-collection procedures.
- Giving program managers sufficient support for data collection to enable them to provide accurate data.
- Accepting a considerable time delay in implementing the measures. Each difficulty of whatever kind can contribute an unusually long delay to the total project.
- Winnowing all possible measures to produce a

much smaller selection of achievable measures. Many more measures of interest will be identified, at least initially, than can be implemented and analyzed.

- Re-examining collection procedures and verifying the data collected shortly after the system is implemented.

- Accepting the fact that costs of the system are difficult to determine, and accurate estimates may be impossible until the system has operated for some time.

BIBLIOGRAPHY

Adams, Stuart. *Evaluative Research in Corrections: A Practical Guide,* Washington, D.C., U.S. Department of Justice, Law Enforcement Assistance Administration, March 1975.

—————————. "Evaluative Research in Corrections: Status and Prospects," *Federal Probation,* 38(1):14, March 1974.

American Bar Association Commission on Correctional Facilities and Services, Resource Center on Correctional Law and Legal Services, *Medical and Health Care in Jails, Prisons, and Other Correctional Facilities: A Compilation of Standards and Materials,* Washington, D.C., American Bar Association, August 1974.

Andenaes, Johannes. "The General Preventive Effects of Punishment," *University of Pennsylvania Law Review,* 114 (No. 7):949, May 1966.

Antunes, George E., and A. Lee Hunt, "The Impact of Certainty and Severity of Punishment on Levels of Crime in American States: An Extended Analysis," Paper presented at the 1974 American Political Science Association Annual Convention.

Bailey, William C., J. David Martin, and Louis N. Gray. "Crime and Deterrence: A Correlational Analysis," *Journal of Research in Crime and Delinquency,* 11(2):124, July 1974.

Baker, Keith, et al. *Summary Report: Project Newgate and Other Prison College Education Programs,* Washington, D.C., Office of Economic Opportunity, April 1973.

Barton, Marlin, and W. O. Jenkins. *The Maladaptive Behavior Record (MBR): A Scale for the Analysis and Prediction of Community Adjustment and Recidivism of Offenders,* Elmore, Alabama, Experimental Manpower Laboratory for Corrections, Rehabilitation Research Foundation, January 1973.

Battle v. *Anderson.* 376 F.Supp. 402 (E.D. Okla.) May 30, 1975.

Bloch, Peter B., and Deborah Anderson. *Policewomen on Patrol: Final Report,* Washington, D.C., Police Foundation, May 1974.

Blumstein, Alfred, and Jacqueline Cohen. "An Evaluation of a College-Level Program in a Maximum Security Prison," Pittsburgh, Pa., Carnegie-Mellon University, Urban Systems Institute, April 1974.

Brooker, Frank. "The Deterrent Effect of Punishment," *Criminology,* February 1972, p. 469.

Brutsche, Robert L. "Problems of Health Care Delivery in Penal Institutions," *New York State Journal of Medicine,* June 1975.

Conrad, John P. "Fifty Years in a Squirrel Cage: The Past, Present, and Future of Evaluation in Corrections," paper presented at the Florida Conference on Evaluation Research, March 11-12, 1976.

—————————. "Never Should Have Promised a Hospital," *Federal Probation,* December 1975.

Cressey, Donald R. "Adult Felons in Prison," in Lloyd E. Ohlin, ed., *Prisoners in America,* American Assembly Series, Englewood Cliffs, N.J., Prentice-Hall, 1973.

Dahlstrom, W. Grant, George Schlager Welsh, and Leona E. Dahlstrom. *An MMPI Handbook.* Clinical Interpretation, vol. 1, rev. ed., University of Minnesota, 1972, *Research Applications,* vol. 2, rev. ed., University of Minnesota, 1975.

"Declaration of Principles of American Correctional

Association, Revised and Reaffirmed in 1960," *Mannual of Correctional Standards,* College Park, Md., American Correctional Association, 1966.

District of Columbia, FY 1975 Budget, Office of the Mayor, Washington, D.C.

Dixon, Michael C., et al. *Juvenile Delinquency Prevention Programs,* Nashville, Tenn., Peabody College for Teachers, October 1974.

Dresden, Donald. "Dining in the D.C. Jail," *Washington Post, Potomac,* June 17, 1973.

Engebretsen, Bery, and J. W. Olson. "Primary Care in a Penal Institution: A Study of Health Care Problems Encountered," *Medical Care* 13(9): 775–81, September 1975.

Enyon, Thomas G., Harry E. Allen, and Walter C. Reckless. "Measuring Impact of a Juvenile Correctional Institution by Perceptions of Inmates and Staff," *Journal of Research in Crime and Delinquency* 8(1), January 1971.

Ericson, Richard C., et al. "The Application of Comprehensive Psycho-social Vocational Services in the Rehabilitation of Parolees: January 1, 1965–December 31, 1965," mimeographed, Minneapolis Rehabilitation Center, January 1966.

Federal Register. 40(167):38771-2. Wednesday, August 27, 1975.

The Future of Corrections, vol. 381, *Annals of the American Academy of Political and Social Science,* January 1969.

Gates v. *Collier,* 349 F.Supp. 881 (N.D. Miss. 1972) off'd. 510 F2d 1291(5th Cir., 1974).

Geismar, Ludwig L. *Family and Community Functioning: A Manual of Measurement for Social Work Practice and Policy.* Metuchen, N.J., Scarecrow Press, 1971.

Glaser, Daniel. *The Effectiveness of a Prison and Parole System,* Indianapolis, Bobbs-Merrill, 1964.

——————,ed. *Handbook of Criminology,* Chicago, Rand McNally, n.d.

——————. "National Goals and Indicators for the Reduction of Crime and Delinquency," *The Annals of the American Academy of Political and Social Science,* vol. 371, May 1967.

——————. "Remedies for the Key Deficiency in Criminal Justice Evaluation Research," *Journal of Research in Crime and Delinquency,* 11(2):144, July 1974.

——————. *Routinizing Evaluation: Getting Feedback on the Effectiveness of Crime and Delinquency Programs,* Washington, D.C., Government Printing Office, 1973.

——————— and Vincent O'Leary, for the National Parole Institutes. *Personal Characteristics and Parole Outcome,* Washington, D.C., U.S. Department of Health, Education and Welfare, Social and Rehabilitation Service, Office of Juvenile Delinquency and Youth Development, 1968.

Goldsmith, Seth B. *Prison Health: A Travesty of Justice,* New York, Prodist, div of Neale Watson Academic Publications, Inc., 1975.

——————. "The Status of Prison Health Care: A Review of the Literature," *Public Health Reports* 89(6):569–75, November/December 1974.

Gottfredson, Don M. "Five Challenges," *Journal of Research in Crime and Delinquency,* 9(2), July 1972.

——————, et al. "4000 Lifetimes: A Study of Time Served and Parole Outcomes," Davis, Calif., National Council on Crime and Delinquency, 1971.

Guenther, Anthony L. "The Forms and Functions of Prison Contraband," *Crime and Delinquency,* vol. 21, no. 3, Davis, Calif., National Council on Crime and Delinquency, July 1975.

Hoffman, Peter B., James L. Beck, and Lucille K. DeGostin. "The Practical Application of a Severity Scale," Parole Decision-Making Supplemental Report Thirteen, Davis, Calif., National Council on Crime and Delinquency, June 1973.

Hood, Roger G. "Research on the Effectiveness of Punishments and Treatments," *Collected Studies in Criminological Research,* vol. 1, Strasbourg, France, European Committee on Crime Problems, Council of Europe, 1967.

——————, and Richard Sparks. *Key Issues in Criminology,* London, World University Library.

Jenkins, W. O., et al. *The Measurement and Prediction of Criminal Behavior and Recidivism: The Environmental Deprivation Scale (EDS) and the Maladaptive Behavior Record (MBR),* Montgomery, Alabama, Experimental Manpower Laboratory for Corrections, Rehabilitation Research Foundation, Alabama Industrial School, December 1972.

Kassebaum, Gene, David Wilner, and David Ward. *Prison Treatment and Parole Survival,* New York, Wiley, 1971.

Kupersmith, G. *High Impact Anti-Crime Program: Sample Impact Project Evaluation Components,* U.S. Department of Justice, Law Enforcement Assistance Administration, Washington, D.C., Government Printing Office, July 1974.

Law Enforcement Assistance Administration. *Criminal Justice Surveys in 13 American Cities.* Washington, D.C., Government Printing Office, 1975.

Lehman, Paul E. "A Medical Model of Treatment," *Crime and Delinquency,* 18(2).

Lejins, Peter P. "Toward Better Knowledge in Corrections," Proceedings of the American Correctional Association Meeting, College Park, Md., American Correctional Association, 1958.

_____, and Thomas F. Courtless. "A General Model for Justification and Evaluation of Correctional Programs," Proceedings of the 103rd Annual Congress of Correction of the American Correctional Association, 1973.

Lenihan, K. J. "When Money Counts: An Experimental Study of Providing Financial Aid and Job Placement Services to Released Offenders," Washington, D.C., Bureau of Social Science Research, 1976 draft report.

Lipton, Douglas; Robert Martinson, and Judith Wilks. The Effectiveness of Correctional Treatment: A Survey of Treatment Evaluation Studies. New York, Praeger, 1975.

Logan, Charles H. "Evaluation Research in Crime and Delinquency: A Reappraisal," The Journal of Criminal Law, Criminology and Political Science, 63(3), September 1972.

Los Angeles Police Department, Criminal Justice Monitoring Unit. California Criminal Justice System Analysis: Mid-Year Report, 1974 (rev. November 1974).

Manual of Correctional Standards, 3rd ed., Washington, D.C., American Correctional Association, 1966.

Martinson, Robert. "What Works?—A Question and Answer About Prison Reform," Public Interest, Spring 1974, pp. 22–54.

Miller, Stuart J., and Simon Dinitz. "Measuring Institutional Impact—A Follow-Up," Criminology 11(3), November 1973.

Moberg, David, and Richard Ericson. "A New Recidivism Outcome Index," Federal Probation, June 1972, pp. 50–57.

Montgomery, Reid. "A Measure of Inmate Satisfaction/Dissatisfaction in Selected South Carolina Institutions," Ph.D. dissertation, University of South Carolina, Columbia, 1974.

Morris, Norval, and Frank Zimring. "Deterrence and Correction," The Annals of the American Academy of Political and Social Science, special edition on The Future of Corrections, vol. 381, January 1969.

National Advisory Commission on Criminal Justice Standards and Goals. Corrections, Washington, D.C., Government Printing Office, 1973.

Newman v. Alabama. 349 F.Supp. 278 (M. C. Ala., 1972).

"1972 Probation and Parole Termination," Statistical Bulletin C-56, Wisconsin Department of Correc-tions, Bureau of Planning, Development, and Research, Madison, October 1973.

North Carolina Department of Correction, Statistical Data in Support of the Budget for FY 1975–77 Biennium. Raleigh, May 1976.

North Carolina Department of Human Resources, Division of Health Services, Sanitary Engineering Section. "Rules and Regulations Governing the Sanitation of Local Confinement Facilities," Raleigh, State Government of North Carolina, Form #409 (rev. January 1972).

Office of Health and Medical Affairs. Key to Health for a Padlocked Society: Design for Health Care in Michigan Prisons, Lansing, Michigan Department of Corrections, 1975.

_____. Key to Health for a Padlocked Society: A Technical Supplement, Lansing, Michigan Department of Corrections, October 1974.

Ohlin, Lloyd E., Harmon Piven, and Donnell M. Pappenfort. "Major Dilemma of the Social Worker in Probation and Parole, National Probation and Parole Association Journal, 2(3): 211–25, July 1956.

Panton, J. H. Interpretive Handbook for the MMPI In Correctional Classification and Diagnostic Services, Raleigh, North Carolina Department of Correction, January 1975.

Protzel, Mary Sue. "Nursing Behind Bars," American Journal of Nursing, 27(3):505–508, March 1972.

Reasons, C. E., and R. L. Kaplan. "Tear Down the Walls? Some Functions of Prison," Crime and Delinquency, October 1975, pp. 360–72.

Reed, James A. "Program Evaluation Research," Federal Probation, 38(1):37, March 1974.

Report to the President's Commission on Law Enforcement and the Administration of Justice, Task Force Report, Washington, D.C., Government Printing Office, 1967.

Rhode Island Department of Corrections. Recidivism at the Adult Correctional Institute, January 1–December 31, 1972: Final Report and January 1–December 31, 1974 Provisional Report, Cranston, R. I., 1975.

Robison, James, and Gerald Smith. "The Effectiveness of Correctional Programs," Crime and Delinquency, 17(1):67, January 1971.

Sellin, T., and M. E. Wolfgang. The Measurement of Delinquency, New York, Wiley. 1964.

Sindwani, K. L., and Walter C. Reckless. "Prisoners' Perceptions of the Impact of Institutional Stay," Criminology, 10(4):February 1974.

Smith, Ralph W., Who Returns? A Study of Recidivism for Adult Offenders in the State of Washington, Department of Social and Health Services,

Planning and Research Division, Olympia, Washington, March 1976.

Sparks, R. F. "Research on the Use and Effectiveness of Probation, Parole, and Measures of After-Care," *Practical Organization of Measures for the Supervision and After-Care of Conditionally Sentenced or Conditionally Released Offenders,* Strasbourg, France, Council of Europe, European Committee on Crime Problems, 1970.

Statewide Jail Standards and Inspection Systems Project. *Survey and Handbook on State Standards and Inspection Legislation for Jails and Juvenile Detention Facilities,* Commission on Correctional Facilities and Services, Washington, D.C., American Bar Association, August 1974.

The Status of Productivity Measurement in State Government: An Initial Examination, Washington, D.C., The Urban Institute, 1975.

Study to Determine the Recidivism Rate for the South Carolina Department of Corrections' Calendar Year 1972 Releases, Division of Planning and Research, Columbia, State of South Carolina, March 22, 1976.

Task Force on Prison and Jail Health, *The Captive Patient: Prison Care in Kentucky,* Lexington, Ky., Kentucky Public Health Association, January 1974.

"Treatment Behind Bars," *Time,* 102:35–6, July 9, 1973.

U.S. Department of Justice, Federal Bureau of Investigation. *Crime in the United States: Uniform Crime Reports—1970,* Washington, D.C., August 31, 1971.

——————. *Crime in the United States: Uniform Crime Reports—1974.* Washington, D.C., November 17, 1975.

U.S. Department of Justice, Law Enforcement Assistance Administration. *Sourcebook of Criminal Justice Statistics, 1974,* Washington, D.C., Government Printing Office, 1974.

Walker, Brian E., Paul Valaer, and Theodore J. Gordon. "Environmental Health Factors in Penal and Correctional Institutions," *Journal of Environmental Health,* 36:270–77, November-December 1973.

Waller, Irving. "Conditional and Unconditional Discharge from Prison: Effects and Effectiveness," *Federal Probation,* 38(2), June 1974.

Wayne County Jail Inmates, et al., v. Wayne County Board of Commissioners, et al., 1 Pr.L.Reptr. 5 Wayne County, Michigan, Cir.Ct. 1971.

Wenk, Ernest, and Rudolph Moos. "Social Climates in Prison: An Attempt to Conceptualize and Measure Environmental Factors in Total Institutions," *Journal of Research in Crime and Delinquency,* 9(2):134–48, July 1972.

——————, and Colin Frank. "Some Progress in the Evaluation of Institutional Programs," *Federal Probation,* 39(3), September 1973.

Wilkins, Leslie T. *Evaluation of Penal Measures,* New York, Random House, 1969.

——————, and P. MacNaughton-Smith. "New Prediction and Classification Methods in Criminology," in *Probation and Parole: Selected Readings,* edited by Robert M. Carter and Leslie T. Wilkins, New York, Wiley, 1970.

Wilson, James Q. "Lock 'Em Up and Other Thoughts on Crime," *New York Times Magazine,* March 9, 1975.

Witherspoon, A. D., E. K. deValera, and W. O. Jenkins. *The Law Encounter Severity Scale (LESS): A Criterion for Criminal Behavior and Recidivism,* Montgomery, Alabama, Experimental Manpower Laboratory for Corrections, Rehabilitation and Research Foundation, August 1973.

Witte, Ann D. "Work Release in North Carolina: An Evaluation of its Effects after Release from Incarceration," Raleigh, North Carolina Department of Correction, 1976.

REPORTS FROM STATE CORRECTIONS AGENCIES

Alabama Board of Corrections. *Financial and Statistical Report, 1974–75.*

Arizona State Department of Corrections. *Arizona Correctional Statistics, 1974.*

Colorado Department of Institutions, Division of Correctional Services, Office of Research and Planning. *Statistical Trends Section of the First Year Plan and Budget Request, Fiscal Year 1976–1977.*

Connecticut Department of Correction. *Annual Report, 1974.*

——————. *Statistical Summary, End of Quarter 1,* March 31, 1976.

Florida Division of Corrections. *Annual Report, 1973–74.*

Georgia Department of Corrections and Offender Rehabilitation. *Annual Report, 1974.*

——————. *Annual Report, 1975* (draft report).

Illinois Department of Corrections. *Annual Report, Fiscal Year 1975.*

Indiana Department of Correction. *The Annual Abstract of the Department of Correction, 1972–1973.*

Kansas Board of Probation and Parole. *1974 Biennial Report.*

Louisiana Department of Corrections. *Annual Statistical Report, Fiscal Year 1973–1974.*

Maryland Division of Correction. *Forty-Sixth Report, Fiscal Year 1974.*

Massachusetts Department of Correction. *An Analysis of Recidivism Among Residents Released from Massachusetts Correctional Institutions During the Year 1972 in Comparison with Releases in the Years 1966 and 1971,* March 1976.

Michigan Office of the Auditor General. *Audit Report: Corrections Camp Program, Department of Corrections, October 1, 1970 through January 31, 1973.*

Michigan Department of Corrections. *Annual Report, 1974.*

Minnesota Department of Corrections. *Biennial Report, '71–73.*

Missouri Division of Corrections. *Annual Status Report, July 1, 1973–July 1, 1974.*

Nebraska Department of Correctional Services. *Annual Report, 1974–1975.*

New Hampshire State Prison. *Report of the Officers of the New Hampshire State Prison for the Two Years Ending June 30, 1972.* Concord, New Hampshire.

New Jersey Department of Institutions and Agencies, Correctional Master Plan Project. *Profile of State Institution Offenders, Fiscal 1970–1975.*

New Mexico Department of Corrections. *Annual Report, 63rd Fiscal Year, July 1, 1974 through June 30, 1975.*

New York Department of Correctional Services. *Annual Report, 1974.*

——————. *Annual Statistical Report, 1974 Data: Inmate and Parole Populations.*

North Dakota. *Third Biennial Report of the Director of Institutions to the Governor. Period of Report: July 1, 1973 to June 30, 1975.*

Ohio Department of Rehabilitation and Correction. *Annual Report, Fiscal Year 1975.*

——————. *Report of the Ohio Department of Rehabilitation and Correction, May, 1974.*

Oklahoma Corrections Department. *Annual Report for Fiscal Years 1974 and 1975.*

Rhode Island Department of Corrections. *Evaluation of Adult Education Programs at the Rhode Island Adult Correctional Institution, August 1973 through March 1976.*

South Carolina Department of Corrections. *Annual Report of the Board of Corrections and the Director of the South Carolina Department of Corrections for the Period July 1, 1973 to June 30, 1974.*

——————. *Quarterly Statistical Report. Second Quarter, FY 1976.*

——————. *Standards for City Jails and Overnight Lockups,* October 1972.

——————. *Standards for County Jails,* October 1972.

——————. *Standards for County Prisons,* October 1972.

Tennessee Department of Correction. *Annual Report, 1973–1974.*

Texas Department of Corrections. *1975 Annual Statistical Report.*

Virginia Department of Corrections. *1974–1975. Annual Report.*

Washington Department of Social and Health Services, Division of Adult Corrections—Institutions. *Quarterly Client Characteristic and Population Movement Report, April–June 1976.*

West Virginia Commissioner of Public Institutions. *Annual Report, July 1, 1973 to June 30, 1974.*

Wyoming Governor's Planning Committee on Criminal Administration. *Criminal Justice System Data Book—1974.*

Wyoming Board of Charities and Reform. *1975 Annual Report of the Board of Charities and Reform, July 1, 1974 through June 30, 1975.*